DECREE AND BE ESTABLISHED

Prophetic Declarations for Every Area of Life

Francisca Okeya

TABLE OF CONTENTS

DEDICATION

To the One who speaks, and it is done, The God of all power, the Word made flesh, my source and sustainer, this book is dedicated to You, Lord Jesus Christ, for teaching me the power of prophetic declaration and the authority of the spoken word.

To the Holy Spirit, my constant teacher and helper, thank You for divine inspiration, insight, and utterance.

To everyone who dares to believe that life and death are in the power of the tongue, may these declarations shape your destiny, shift your atmosphere, and ignite your faith.

And to every intercessor, believer, and warrior who refuses to be silent in the face of adversity this is for you. May your mouth never run dry of fire, and may your voice always establish heaven's will on earth.

ACKNOWLEDGMENT

I give all glory to the Lord Jesus Christ, the Living Word, who empowers and anoints every decree that aligns with His truth. Without His Spirit, this book would be mere words, but with Him, it becomes a weapon of transformation and breakthrough.

To the Holy Spirit, my Teacher, Comforter, and Guide, honour You. Thank You for every revelation, whisper, and prompting that birthed these declarations. You are the true Author of this work.

To all the intercessors, prayer warriors, and faith-filled believers who inspired this journey, thank you for showing what it means to live boldly and speak with authority. Your lives are living testimonies of the power of prophetic declaration.

To my family and loved ones, your unwavering support, patience, and prayers gave me strength during the writing process.

To the countless readers, ministers, and believers around the world who have been hungering for spiritual empowerment, this book is for you. May these declarations unlock victories, restore destinies, and stir revival in every area of your life.

With love, honour, and gratitude,

Francisca Okeya

INTRODUCTION

Words are powerful. They are not just sounds; they are spiritual containers, filled with life or death, faith or fear, breakthrough or bondage. From the beginning of time, God created the world with words. He said, "Let there be," and it was so (Genesis 1). As children of God, made in His image, we carry that same creative authority through the words we speak.

This book was birthed out of a divine revelation: that believers are not meant to live as victims of circumstances, but as victorious sons and daughters who legislate Heaven's will on Earth. The enemy thrives in silence and passivity, but when a believer opens their mouth to decree the Word of God in faith, the atmosphere must shift. Angels are dispatched. Mountains move. Chains break. Destinies are realigned.

Decree and Be Established: Prophetic Declarations for Every Area of Life is your weapon of warfare and tool of transformation. Each chapter targets a specific area of life, from spiritual growth, healing, and finances, to deliverance, marriage, divine protection, and more. Within each chapter, you will find 20 powerful, Spirit-breathed declarations that begin with "I decree" or "I declare" and end with "in Jesus' name." These are not mere affirmations. They are prophetic pronouncements rooted in Scripture, charged with power, and designed to activate divine intervention.

As you speak to them aloud, do so with boldness. Don't

just repeat the words, believe them. Let them saturate your atmosphere, renew your mind, build your faith, and shape your reality.

According to Job 22:28, "You will also declare a thing, and it will be established for you; so light will shine on your ways."

When you decree God's Word, you're not just expressing hope, you're establishing His will in your life.

You may be facing impossible situations, demonic resistance, or long-standing affliction, but God has given you a voice. Use it. Decree life over death, healing over sickness, open doors over closed ones, and light over darkness.

This is not just a book, it's a spiritual tool. A prophetic trumpet in your hand. A scriptural sword in your mouth.

Get ready to speak boldly. Get ready to see results.

Decree and be established, in Jesus' name.

How To Use This Book Decree And Be Established: Prophetic Declarations For Every Area Of Life

Decree and Be Established is not just a book, it is a prophetic tool designed to shape your life, shift atmospheres, and manifest God's promises through the power of declaration. Each chapter targets a specific area of life, such as healing, Favor, destiny, divine protection, provision, deliverance, and more. These prophetic declarations are written to activate faith, enforce spiritual authority, and align your life with the Word of God.

1. Understand The Power Of Decrees

Declarations are not mere words; they are spiritual commands spoken with divine backing. Job 22:28 (NKJV) says:

"You will also declare a thing, and it will be established for you; so light will shine on your ways."

When you decree according to God's will, you give heaven permission to move on your behalf. These declarations help you enforce what is already yours through Christ.

2. Speak With Boldness And Authority

This book is meant to be spoken aloud. Don't whisper, declare each prophetic word with authority, like a king giving orders. Ecclesiastes 8:4 (NKJV) says:

"Where the word of a king is, there is power..."

As a child of God, your declarations carry weight in the spirit realm. Let your voice echo what heaven has already decreed.

3. Use It Daily Or Thematically

You can use this book in two ways:
- Daily: Declare a few declarations from different chapters as part of your morning or evening routine.
- Topically: Focus on a specific chapter that aligns with your current situation, such as healing, breakthrough, or open doors, and speak all 20 declarations repeatedly until you see change.

Isaiah 55:11 (NKJV) confirms:

"So shall My word be that goes forth from My mouth; it shall not return to Me void..."

4. Combine Declarations With Fasting And Prayer

During times of fasting, use the declarations as powerful weapons to intensify your spiritual engagement. Speak them before or after your prayer time, combining faith with focus. This aligns with Mark 11:23 (NKJV):

"Whoever says to this mountain, 'Be removed and be cast into the sea,' and does not doubt...he will have whatever he says."

5. Use It In Spiritual Warfare And Breakthrough Moments

When facing stubborn battles, delays, or demonic

resistance, speak the declarations repeatedly with persistence. The declarations in this book will serve as your sword against the enemy.

Jeremiah 23:29 (NKJV) says:

"Is not My word like a fire," says the Lord, "and like a hammer that breaks the rock in pieces?"

6. Read Aloud Over Loved Ones And Situations

You can personalize the declarations for family members, friends, your ministry, business, or nation. Speak over their lives as an intercessor and prophetic vessel. Your words can bring transformation. Proverbs 18:21 (NKJV) reminds us:

"Death and life are in the power of the tongue, and those who love it will eat its fruit."

Final Encouragement

This is not a book to read once and put away, it is a spiritual resource to return to again and again. As you decree, heaven will establish. As you speak, angels will act. As you prophesy, chains will break, and miracles will manifest. Let your mouth be God's instrument and watch your world shift in Jesus' name.

CHAPTER 1

Spiritual Growth &
Intimacy with God

According to Job 22:28, "You will also declare a thing, and it will be established for you; so light will shine on your ways."

Spiritual growth and intimacy with God are the foundation of every victorious Christian life. When we grow spiritually, we become more like Christ in character, wisdom, and power. Intimacy with God is not reserved for a select few, it is God's desire for all His children to walk closely with Him, hear His voice, and live in constant fellowship.

God is calling us deeper. He longs for a relationship where we don't just seek His hand but also seek His face. As you grow in your knowledge of Him, your confidence in His promises increases. The more time you spend with God, the more you are transformed into His image and equipped to fulfil your divine purpose.

Prophetic declarations are powerful tools in building spiritual momentum. When you speak God's Word over your life, your spirit is strengthened, your atmosphere is shifted, and the forces of darkness are pushed back. As you declare truth over your life, faith rises and intimacy with God deepens. Declarations align your words with heaven's will.

Let this chapter stir your hunger for God. Use these declarations to call forth spiritual maturity, deeper hunger for His Word, and consistent communion with the Holy Spirit.

Key Scriptures:

- "Draw near to God and He will draw near to you." James 4:8 (NKJV)
- "But grow in the grace and knowledge of our Lord and Savior Jesus Christ." 2 Peter 3:18 (NKJV)
- "As the deer pants for the water brooks, so pants my soul for You, O God." Psalm 42:1 (NKJV)
- "Blessed are those who hunger and thirst for righteousness, for they shall be filled." Matthew 5:6 (NKJV)
- You shall also decree a thing, and it shall be established for you; so light will shine on your ways." Job 22:28 (NKJV)

Prophetic Declarations

1. I decree that my spirit is awakened to the voice of the Holy Spirit, and I walk in deep fellowship with God daily, refusing to be distracted or disconnected from His presence, in Jesus' name.
2. I decree that I hunger and thirst for righteousness more than ever before, and my soul is satisfied with the richness of God's Word and the overflow of His Spirit, in Jesus' name.
3. I decree that my heart is tender and teachable

11

before God, and I receive divine instructions with joy, obeying without hesitation and growing in wisdom, in Jesus' name.

4. I decree that the fire of the Holy Ghost burns continually upon the altar of my heart, keeping me fervent, focused, and faithful in my walk with God, in Jesus' name.

5. I decree that the eyes of my understanding are enlightened, and I grasp the mysteries of the Kingdom with clarity and boldness, walking in divine revelation, in Jesus' name.

6. I decree that my spiritual ears are open to God's frequency, and I will not miss His direction, instruction, or correction, for I walk closely with Him daily, in Jesus' name.

7. I decree that every scale of spiritual blindness is removed from my life, and I see God, His Word, and my destiny through His light and not through the lens of the flesh, in Jesus' name.

8. I decree that I grow in grace and in the knowledge of my Lord Jesus Christ, maturing in character, discernment, and love, in Jesus' name.

9. I decree that my prayer life is alive, powerful, and consistent, and I tarry in the secret place until I am transformed by His glory, in Jesus' name.

10. I decree that I abide in Christ and His words abide in me, and because of this unbreakable connection, I bear much fruit that glorifies the Father, in Jesus' name.

11. I decree that I walk in step with the Holy Spirit, yielding completely to His promptings, and I do not grieve or quench Him in any area of my life,

in Jesus' name.

12. I decree that I am full of spiritual understanding and divine discernment, and I am never deceived by the tactics of the enemy, in Jesus' name.

13. I decree that my life is saturated with the presence of God, and everywhere I go, I carry His glory and manifest His character, in Jesus' name.

14. I decree that I am rooted and grounded in the love of Christ, and nothing can separate me from the love of God that is in Christ Jesus my Lord, in Jesus' name.

15. I decree that the Word of God dwells richly in me, shaping my thoughts, renewing my mind, and guiding my actions daily, in Jesus' name.

16. I decree that I love what God loves and hate what He hates, and I pursue holiness with passion, resisting every appearance of evil, in Jesus' name.

17. I decree that I am a vessel of honour, set apart for the Master's use, prepared for every good work and filled with His Spirit, in Jesus' name.

18. I decree that I grow daily in spiritual stature, authority, and Favor with God and man, becoming a reflection of Christ to the world, in Jesus' name.

19. I decree that the fruit of the Spirit is evident in my life, and I am marked by love, joy, peace, patience, kindness, goodness, faithfulness, gentleness, and self-control, in Jesus' name.

20. I decree that nothing will separate me from the presence of God, no sin, no situation, no storm,

for I am hidden in Christ and consumed with His presence, in Jesus' name.

CHAPTER 2

Health & Healing

Health and healing are not only physical necessities, but divine provisions secured for every believer through the finished work of Jesus Christ. At the cross, Jesus bore not just our sins but also our sicknesses, pains, and infirmities. Healing is not merely something we hope for, it is something that has already been paid for.

Isaiah 53:5 declares that by His stripes we are healed. Healing encompasses the body, soul, and spirit. God desires that we walk in wholeness and vitality, free from the torment of disease, affliction, and emotional pain. As children of God, we must boldly take hold of what belongs to us through faith-filled words.

Prophetic declarations activate the power of God's promises. Speaking healing over your life aligns your body with divine truth and breaks the lies of sickness and fear. As you decree healing, the atmosphere shifts, your faith rises, and your body responds to the Word of God.

Let your declarations be bold. Refuse to accept sickness as your identity. You are not the sick trying to be healed, you are the healed resisting sickness. Declare healing, restoration, and divine strength until it manifests.

Key Scriptures:

- "But He was wounded for our transgressions, He was bruised for our iniquities… and by His stripes we are healed." Isaiah 53:5 (NKJV)
- "Beloved, I pray that you may prosper in all things and be in health, just as your soul prospers." 3 John 1:2 (NKJV)
- "You shall also decree a thing, and it shall be established for you; so light will shine on your ways." Job 22:28 (NKJV)
- "He sent His word and healed them and delivered them from their destructions." Psalm 107:20

Prophetic Declarations

1. I decree that by the stripes of Jesus, I am completely healed and made whole in every part of my body, soul, and spirit, and no sickness or disease has a legal right to dwell in me, in Jesus' name.

2. I decree that divine health flows through my veins, energizes my body, strengthens my bones, and renews my cells with supernatural vitality, in Jesus' name.

3. I decree that every organ, tissue, and system in my body functions perfectly according to God's original design, and anything contrary to health is uprooted and cast out, in Jesus' name.

4. I decree that the healing virtue of Jesus flows through me now, destroying every trace of illness, infirmity, weakness, and affliction, in Jesus' name.

5. I decree that I walk in the fullness of divine healing, and I reject every medical verdict or negative report that contradicts the finished work of the cross, in Jesus' name.

6. I decree that my body is the temple of the Holy Spirit, and therefore, no sickness, infection, virus, inflammation, or chronic condition can defile or dominate me, in Jesus' name.

7. I decree that healing is my covenant right through the blood of Jesus, and I lay hold of it by faith and walk in complete restoration daily, in Jesus' name.

8. I decree that every generational sickness, hereditary condition, or family diagnosis is broken and reversed in my life by the power of the blood, in Jesus' name.

9. I decree that the same Spirit that raised Jesus from the dead quickens my mortal body, renewing my strength like the eagle's and empowering me to run and not grow weary, in Jesus' name.

10. I decree that I am emotionally healed from every trauma, disappointment, grief, and mental burden, and I receive the peace and comfort of the Holy Spirit, in Jesus' name.

11. I decree that every hidden sickness or undiagnosed condition is exposed, uprooted, and destroyed before it can take root, in Jesus' name.

12. I decree that my immune system is divinely strengthened, and no sickness or plague shall come near my dwelling, for the Lord is my shield

and fortress, in Jesus' name.

13. I decree that healing flows to every area of pain, stiffness, or malfunction in my body, and I receive total relief and restoration now, in Jesus' name.

14. I decree that I am free from cycles of medication, hospital visits, and medical fear, and I step into a new season of supernatural health and wholeness, in Jesus' name.

15. I decree that I will live and not die, and I will declare the works of the Lord, fulfilling every purpose He ordained for me in divine strength, in Jesus' name.

16. I decree that every demonic spirit of infirmity sent to afflict my body is bound and cast out now by the authority of the name of Jesus, in Jesus' name.

17. I decree that my mind is healed, my emotions are stabilized, and I have the mind of Christ, clear, peaceful, and full of life, in Jesus' name.

18. I decree that divine health is my portion every day of my life, and I rise with renewed strength and supernatural energy each morning, in Jesus' name.

19. I decree that every report of the enemy concerning my health is nullified, reversed, and rendered powerless, and only the Word of God shall stand, in Jesus' name.

20. I decree that healing is flowing from the crown of my head to the soles of my feet, and I walk boldly in perfect health, giving glory to God, in Jesus' name.

CHAPTER 3

Financial Prosperity & Provision

Financial prosperity is not just about accumulating wealth; it is about stepping into the abundance God has already provided and living as a steward of His kingdom resources. God is not limited in supply, and He delights in blessing His children so they can be a blessing to others. Provision is part of our covenant inheritance through Christ.

In Deuteronomy 8:18, we are reminded that it is God who gives us the power to get wealth. When we align our hearts with His purpose and obey His instructions, He releases provision, open doors, and supernatural Favor. Your financial situation is not permanent; it can shift when you align your words and faith with the promises of God.

Prophetic declarations have the power to break the spirit of lack and usher in divine provision. As you decree abundance, open doors, and debt cancellation, you are not just speaking positive words, you are activating spiritual laws that respond to faith-filled utterance. Your words set things in motion.

Stand on the truth that you are not created to live in lack or struggle. Declare breakthrough in your finances. Speak life over your business, job, and financial destiny. Heaven responds when you declare with boldness and faith.

Key Scriptures:

- "You shall remember the Lord your God, for it is He who gives you power to get wealth..." Deuteronomy 8:18 (NKJV)
- "The young lions lack and suffer hunger; but those who seek the Lord shall not lack any good thing." Psalm 34:10 (NKJV)
- "You shall also decree a thing, and it shall be established for you; so light will shine on your ways." Job 22:28 (NKJV)
- "And my God shall supply all your need according to His riches in glory by Christ Jesus." Philippians 4:19 (NKJV)
-

Prophetic Declarations

1. I decree that I am a covenant child of God, and because I serve Jehovah Jireh, I will never lack any good thing, for divine provision is my portion, in Jesus' name.

2. I decree that every financial limitation is broken over my life, and I walk in supernatural abundance, overflow, and more than enough, in Jesus' name.

3. I decree that the windows of heaven are open over me, and blessings are being poured into my life in such measure that I cannot contain them, in Jesus' name.

4. I decree that the wealth of the wicked is laid up for me, and I receive divine transfer, Favor, and increase in unexpected ways, in Jesus' name.

5. I decree that I am a faithful steward of God's resources, and because I honour Him with my substance, my storehouses are full and my harvest is overflowing, in Jesus' name.

6. I decree that financial doors are opening for me speedily, and I am stepping into new realms of prosperity and kingdom wealth, in Jesus' name.

7. I decree that I am the head and not the tail, above only and not beneath, and I lend to nations and never borrow in desperation, in Jesus' name.

8. I decree that I am a Sower of seed into fertile ground, and every seed I plant multiplies and returns to me with divine interest and multiplied Favor, in Jesus' name.

9. I decree that I am surrounded by divine opportunities, profitable ventures, and open doors of provision that no man can shut, in Jesus' name.

10. I decree that the spirit of poverty, debt, and financial stagnation is broken over my life and bloodline, and I walk in the liberty of kingdom wealth, in Jesus' name.

11. I decree that wisdom, knowledge, and divine strategy rest upon me to manage wealth, build lasting prosperity, and create generational blessings, in Jesus' name.

12. I decree that I am free from the fear of not having enough, and I trust fully in God's

unfailing supply, knowing that He takes care of all my needs, in Jesus' name.

13. I decree that unexpected checks, favourable business contracts, profitable partnerships, and divine surprises are locating me now, in Jesus' name.

14. I decree that every financial curse, embargo, or limitation working against my destiny is broken by the power in the blood of Jesus, in Jesus' name.

15. I decree that I attract financial Favor, divine helpers, and supernatural resources that align with my calling and destiny, in Jesus' name.

16. I decree that I am not enslaved by debt or economic fear, for I serve the God who owns the cattle on a thousand hills and supplies abundantly, in Jesus' name.

17. I decree that my finances are covered by the blood of Jesus, and no devourer, thief, or demonic interference can touch what God has blessed me with, in Jesus' name.

18. I decree that I live in the overflow, giving generously, blessing others, funding kingdom work, and walking in supernatural prosperity, in Jesus' name.

19. I decree that I am positioned in the path of divine wealth and led by the Spirit to opportunities that bring increase and honour to God, in Jesus' name.

20. I decree that financial testimonies, breakthroughs, and abundance are manifesting in my life daily, and I shall never

know lack again, in Jesus' name.

CHAPTER 4

Freedom from Cage and
Spiritual Prison

Many believers today are spiritually confined, trapped in invisible prisons that limit progress, joy, and destiny. These spiritual cages can manifest as stagnation, fear, rejection, repetitive failure, or an inability to move forward despite effort. But the good news is this: Jesus came to set the captives free. No power of darkness can keep you bound when the authority of Christ is applied.

Spiritual prisons are often established through covenants, sins, curses, or satanic agreements. But the blood of Jesus is the key that opens every locked gate. When you recognize your authority as a child of God and boldly decree your release, chains break, and prison doors swing open.

Prophetic declarations act like spiritual hammers that break bars of iron and open up gates that have held you captive. As you speak forth God's Word, your voice becomes a weapon of deliverance. This chapter equips you to confront every spiritual prison with boldness, break free, and walk into your divine liberty.

You were not created to be caged. You were redeemed to soar. Begin to speak your way out of every spiritual confinement. Your declarations, made in faith, will enforce your release and establish your dominion in Christ.

Key Scriptures:

- "He brought them out of darkness and the shadow of death and broke their chains in pieces." Psalm 107:14 (NKJV)
- "To open blind eyes, to bring out prisoners from the prison, those who sit in darkness from the prison house." Isaiah 42:7 (NKJV)
- "You shall also decree a thing, and it shall be established for you; so light will shine on your ways." Job 22:28 (NKJV)
- "The Spirit of the Lord is upon Me... to proclaim liberty to the captives and the opening of the prison to those who are bound." Isaiah 61:1 (NKJV)

Prophetic Declarations

1. I decree that every spiritual cage holding my destiny, progress, and potential is shattered by the power of God, in Jesus' name.
2. I decree that I am released from every invisible chain, satanic confinement, or spiritual prison working against my divine assignment, in Jesus' name.
3. I decree that the doors of my liberty are opened, and I walk boldly into the fullness of my purpose, in Jesus' name.
4. I decree that every demonic limitation placed on

my life, voice, influence, or movement is broken and reversed, in Jesus' name.

5. I decree that I break free from every satanic embargo that has restricted my advancement spiritually, financially, emotionally, or physically, in Jesus' name.

6. I decree that my spirit, soul, and body are loosed from every confinement of fear, guilt, trauma, and bondage, in Jesus' name.

7. I decree that the light of God shines into every dark place where I've been held captive, exposing and destroying all works of darkness, in Jesus' name.

8. I decree that every cage of delay, disappointment, and disgrace designed to hold me back is consumed by Holy Ghost fire, in Jesus' name.

9. I decree that I come out of every pit, prison, or place of spiritual suffocation and step into divine liberty and fresh breath, in Jesus' name.

10. I decree that my dreams, gifts, and God-given identity locked away by the enemy are restored and released by divine authority, in Jesus' name.

11. I decree that the same God who loosed Peter from prison sends His angelic help to release me from every spiritual confinement, in Jesus' name.

12. I decree that I am not a victim of spiritual oppression, I rise with power, liberty, and boldness to fulfil my divine assignment, in Jesus' name.

13. I decree that no curse, ritual, or demonic contract can hold me in bondage, for the anointing breaks every yoke, in Jesus' name.

14. I decree that I move from limitation to elevation, from restriction to release, and from captivity to celebration, in Jesus' name.

15. I decree that my mind is free from the lies of the enemy, my emotions are free from wounds, and my body is free from oppression, in Jesus' name.

16. I decree that every prison gate holding my marriage, finances, ministry, or children is broken open, and I walk out in victory, in Jesus' name.

17. I decree that my voice will no longer be silenced, my potential will no longer be caged, and my influence will no longer be buried, in Jesus' name.

18. I decree that I am seated with Christ in heavenly places, far above captivity, witchcraft, and manipulation, in Jesus' name.

19. I decree that every prison warden assigned to monitor and restrict my destiny is arrested by the fire of God, in Jesus' name.

20. I decree that I am free, completely and eternally free, by the power of the cross and the blood of Jesus Christ, in Jesus' name.

CHAPTER 5

Marriage

Marriage is a sacred covenant designed by God to reflect His love, unity, and purpose. It is not just a social institution; it is a divine relationship through which God reveals His glory and blesses generations. However, because of its divine significance, marriage is often a battleground. Many homes are under attack facing division, delay, frustration, infidelity, and barrenness. The good news is that God is still the Author of marriage, and His Word holds the power to build, restore, and bless every union.

Prophetic declarations concerning marriage are powerful because they align your words with God's will and activate His promises. Whether you are believing for a godly spouse, trusting God to heal a broken relationship, or desiring peace in your home, your mouth must partner with your faith. When you decree restoration, unity, and love, the spiritual realm responds.

God desires that your marriage be fruitful, joyful, and built upon Christ. His Word offers protection against the enemy's attacks, healing for wounds, and wisdom for daily living. Through declarations, you not only prophesy life over your marriage, you also uproot every seed of discord and disappointment the enemy has planted.

Let your words create what you want to see in your marriage. If you're unmarried, begin speaking into your future now. If you're married, declare the peace and unity you desire. God watches over His Word to perform it.

Key Scriptures:

- "He who finds a wife finds a good thing and obtains Favor from the Lord." Proverbs 18:22 (NKJV)
- "Therefore, what God has joined together, let not man separate." Mark 10:9 (NKJV)
- "Two are better than one, because they have a good reward for their labour." Ecclesiastes 4:9 (NKJV)
- "You shall also decree a thing, and it shall be established for you..." Job 22:28 (NKJV)

Prophetic Declarations

1. I decree that my marriage is built on the solid rock of Christ, unshakable by storms, trials, or attacks, and firmly established in covenant love, in Jesus' name.
2. I decree that my spouse and I walk in unity, agreement, and mutual respect, and we honour each other as vessels of God's purpose, in Jesus' name.
3. I decree that the love between my spouse and I grows deeper, stronger, and more intimate each day, and no outside influence shall come between us, in Jesus' name.

4. I decree that our communication is seasoned with grace, truth, and understanding, and every wall of silence, misunderstanding, or offense is torn down now, in Jesus' name.

5. I decree that every hidden agenda of the enemy against my marriage is exposed and destroyed, and my home is a place of peace, safety, and joy, in Jesus' name.

6. I decree that my marriage is fruitful spiritually, emotionally, and physically, and every delay, barrenness, or hindrance is reversed by divine intervention, in Jesus' name.

7. I decree that we are spiritually aligned, praying together, growing together, and advancing the kingdom of God in unity and power, in Jesus' name.

8. I decree that my spouse is protected, favoured, and anointed, and I declare that we uplift, support, and encourage one another in every season, in Jesus' name.

9. I decree that every spirit of adultery, lust, deception, or emotional entanglement is cut off from our marriage, and we walk in purity and loyalty, in Jesus' name.

10. I decree that our marriage is a testimony of God's faithfulness, a beacon of light to others, and a holy example of Christ and His Church, in Jesus' name.

11. I decree that the fire of love, passion, and intimacy is rekindled in our union, and we are emotionally connected and attentive to each other's needs, in Jesus' name.

12. I decree that we are in one accord concerning our finances, family, goals, and future, and we move forward as a powerful, unified team, in Jesus' name.

13. I decree that every curse, pattern of divorce, separation, or abuse from our bloodline is broken, and our marriage is free, whole, and blessed, in Jesus' name.

14. I decree that I am a godly spouse, wise, patient, loving, and prayerful, and I serve my partner with joy and humility, in Jesus' name.

15. I decree that our marriage is covered by the blood of Jesus and surrounded by a hedge of divine protection from all forms of evil and intrusion, in Jesus' name.

16. I decree that we speak life into each other and over our home, and the words we release build and not destroy, heal and not wound, strengthen and not divide, in Jesus' name.

17. I decree that our children and descendants will rise and call our marriage blessed, for we have laid a foundation of love, honour, and godliness, in Jesus' name.

18. I decree that every past hurt, offense, or betrayal is healed by the power of God, and we walk in total forgiveness, restoration, and peace, in Jesus' name.

19. I decree that our marriage will not be ordinary, but extraordinary, filled with testimonies, divine provision, kingdom impact, and supernatural joy, in Jesus' name.

20. I decree that my spouse and I will finish strong together, fulfilling our purpose, growing in grace, and glorifying God every step of the way, in Jesus' name.

CHAPTER 6

Children & Future Generations

Children are a heritage from the Lord, a precious gift entrusted to parents for divine purpose and destiny. Beyond just giving birth, God calls parents and caregivers to raise children in His ways, speak life over them, and secure their futures in the realm of the Spirit. In a world full of confusion, rebellion, and demonic distractions, children need covering, guidance, and prophetic direction now more than ever.

As believers, we must not be passive about the destiny of our children. Prophetic declarations help secure their path in life. Whether your children are toddlers or adults, whether they are walking with the Lord or have strayed, your voice as a parent or intercessor carries power. Speak the promises of God over them. Declare divine purpose, protection, and excellence. Even if you do not yet have children, you can prophesy over your future seed and generations to come.

God is a generational God. He made promises to Abraham that stretched to Isaac, Jacob, and beyond. What you declare now sets a foundation for those who come after you. Speak blessings, identity, purity, and obedience over your lineage. Cancel curses, addictions, premature death, and rebellion from operating in their lives.

Every child connected to you shall rise and shine in their generation as you decree God's Word with boldness and faith. The seed of the righteous shall be mighty upon the earth!

Key Scriptures:

- "Children are a heritage from the Lord; the fruit of the womb is a reward." Psalm 127:3 (NKJV)
- "All your children shall be taught by the Lord, and great shall be the peace of your children." Isaiah 54:13 (NKJV)
- "The generation of the upright will be blessed." Psalm 112:2 (NKJV)
- "You shall also decree a thing, and it shall be established for you..." Job 22:28 (NKJV)
-

Prophetic Declarations

1. I decree that my children and descendants are blessed, favoured, and chosen by God, and they will fulfil their divine destinies without delay or deviation, in Jesus' name.

2. I decree that my children are taught of the Lord, and great is their peace, wisdom, and spiritual understanding from an early age, in Jesus' name.

3. I decree that the hand of the Lord is upon my children, marking them for signs and wonders in their generation, and they shall rise as leaders and light-bearers, in Jesus' name.

4. I decree that no evil shall befall my children;

they are shielded from every form of danger, abuse, sickness, and satanic attack, in Jesus' name.

5. I decree that my children excel in knowledge, Favor, and grace, and they stand out for godliness, integrity, and excellence in every environment, in Jesus' name.

6. I decree that every generational curse, ancestral bondage, or negative pattern is broken off my children, and they are free to walk in divine purpose and blessing, in Jesus' name.

7. I decree that my children are filled with the Holy Spirit, walking in truth, purity, and discernment, rejecting every ungodly influence and embracing the ways of the Lord, in Jesus' name.

8. I decree that my children will not be entangled with wrong relationships but are divinely connected to friends and mentors who sharpen and support their calling, in Jesus' name.

9. I decree that the voice of the enemy is silenced over my children, and they hear and follow the voice of the Holy Spirit alone, in Jesus' name.

10. I decree that my children are emotionally whole, mentally sound, and full of joy, hope, and courage to face every season of life, in Jesus' name.

11. I decree that my children will marry right, build godly homes, and raise families rooted in righteousness, legacy, and purpose, in Jesus' name.

12. I decree that my sons are mighty in the land, and

my daughters are virtuous, graceful, and full of wisdom, and they will all be pillars in the house of the Lord, in Jesus' name.

13. I decree that my children are not victims of addiction, rebellion, or confusion, but walk in self-control, clarity, and divine direction, in Jesus' name.

14. I decree that every academic, creative, and spiritual gift within my children is activated, refined, and used to glorify God and advance His kingdom, in Jesus' name.

15. I decree that the plans of God for my children shall prevail, and every demonic interference, sabotage, or delay is destroyed now, in Jesus' name.

16. I decree that I will not mourn over my children, for they will live long, fruitful, and impactful lives that bring joy to heaven and honour to our family, in Jesus' name.

17. I decree that my children are arrows in the hand of the Lord, strong, accurate, and effective, and they shall hit their targets in life and destiny, in Jesus' name.

18. I decree that the legacy of faith, prayer, honour, and righteousness is passed down through me to every generation after me, in Jesus' name.

19. I decree that my children shall be ten times better than their peers, distinguished by the Spirit of excellence, and always favoured among many, in Jesus' name.

20. I decree that from generation to generation, my bloodline will serve the Lord, walk in the Spirit,

and shine as lights in a dark world, in Jesus' name.

CHAPTER 7

Career, Business & Work

Your work is not just a means of earning a living, it is a platform for divine impact, influence, and provision. Whether you are employed, running a business, seeking a job, or still discovering your path, God has a unique plan for your career and productivity. As a believer, your labour is blessed, and your hands are anointed to prosper.

However, many face spiritual resistance in the area of work, delays in promotion, business failure, job loss, financial dryness, or confusion about career direction. These are not always natural problems. They can be rooted in spiritual forces meant to limit destiny fulfilment. That's why it is crucial to speak prophetic declarations over your work life.

Declarations rooted in God's Word help break limitations and release divine Favor, strategy, and elevation. They stir your faith, open heavenly doors, and align your earthly efforts with heaven's blueprint. Speak increase over your business, excellence in your skills, and divine Favor with employers or clients. Let every curse of stagnation or toil without reward be reversed by your faith-filled decrees.

God wants His children to be the head and not the tail, shining examples of diligence, integrity, and success. As you declare His promises over your work, expect open doors, unusual wisdom, and divine appointments.

Remember, your voice sets the pace for your future.

Key Scriptures:

- "You shall remember the Lord your God, for it is He who gives you power to get wealth." Deuteronomy 8:18 (NKJV)
- "Let the Lord be magnified, who has pleasure in the prosperity of His servant." Psalm 35:27 (NKJV)
- "Commit your work to the Lord, and your plans will succeed." Proverbs 16:3 (NLT)
- "You shall also decree a thing, and it shall be established for you..." Job 22:28 (NKJV)

Prophetic Declarations

1. I decree that the work of my hands is blessed, and I excel in my career and business as a vessel of excellence, purpose, and divine Favor, in Jesus' name.
2. I decree that every idea, skill, and gift within me is awakened and aligned with divine opportunities that lead to promotion, growth, and financial increase, in Jesus' name.
3. I decree that I operate with divine wisdom, strategy, and innovation that sets me apart in my field, and I am positioned for success and distinction, in Jesus' name.
4. I decree that doors of opportunity, influence,

and advancement are opening for me now, and I walk boldly through every door God has ordained, in Jesus' name.

5. I decree that I am surrounded by Favor in the workplace, with supervisors, clients, and colleagues, and I rise above every opposition or limitation, in Jesus' name.

6. I decree that every spirit of stagnation, delay, and closed doors is broken off my career and business, and I step into accelerated progress and divine lifting, in Jesus' name.

7. I decree that I am anointed to create wealth, manage resources, and make sound decisions that lead to prosperity and impact for God's kingdom, in Jesus' name.

8. I decree that my business attracts the right clients, connections, and resources, and I operate with integrity, value, and kingdom purpose, in Jesus' name.

9. I decree that my hands are skilled, my mind is sharp, and my attitude is excellent, attracting continuous promotion and open doors in every assignment, in Jesus' name.

10. I decree that I do not labour in vain, and every seed I have sown in my work or business brings forth a multiplied harvest of breakthroughs and rewards, in Jesus' name.

11. I decree that I am free from the fear of failure, workplace intimidation, and performance anxiety, and I walk in boldness, competence, and confidence, in Jesus' name.

12. I decree that every evil plan to sabotage my

work, delay my business growth, or hinder my progress is exposed and destroyed by fire, in Jesus' name.

13. I decree that divine helpers, mentors, and strategic alliances locate me in my profession and business journey, in Jesus' name.

14. I decree that I have clarity, creativity, and courage to take bold steps, seize opportunities, and expand into new territories of influence and success, in Jesus' name.

15. I decree that I am a solution-bearer, a difference-maker, and a light in my field, and my work brings glory to God and impact to others, in Jesus' name.

16. I decree that my resume, proposals, products, and services carry the fragrance of Favor, and I am chosen above others by divine orchestration, in Jesus' name.

17. I decree that my career and business are platforms for kingdom influence, and I do everything with excellence as unto the Lord, in Jesus' name.

18. I decree that I rise above every financial struggle, workplace conflict, and toxic environment, and I operate in divine peace and stability, in Jesus' name.

19. I decree that every failure, loss, or delay in my past is turned into a testimony of restoration, promotion, and supernatural acceleration, in Jesus' name.

20. I decree that my career and business fulfil God's purpose, bless generations, and prosper

continually with divine backing, in Jesus' name.

CHAPTER 8

Divine Protection & Safety

We live in a world filled with danger, visible and invisible. From accidents and violence to spiritual attacks and environmental hazards, the enemy constantly seeks to steal, kill, and destroy. But as a child of God, you are not left defenceless. You have divine protection through the covenant of the blood of Jesus, angelic covering, and God's unbreakable promises.

Prophetic declarations activate and enforce your spiritual security. When you speak the Word of God over your life, family, and environment, you create a shield of divine fire. Declarations remind every opposing force that you are untouchable, hidden under the shadow of the Almighty.

The enemy may plan evil, but it shall not prosper when you boldly declare God's protection. These declarations will reinforce your trust in God's safety, establish divine boundaries, and frustrate the operations of wickedness against your life. They will also speak preservation into your journeys, your home, your sleep, and your daily routines.

You are not alone or unguarded. God has assigned angels to keep you. You are surrounded by divine forces more powerful than any demonic trap. As you speak, declare, and believe, you release heaven's army to fight for you and keep you safe. Don't just hope for protection, declare it! Your words create your covering.

Key Scriptures:

- "No weapon formed against you shall prosper..." Isaiah 54:17 (NKJV)
- "He who dwells in the secret place of the Most High shall abide under the shadow of the Almighty." Psalm 91:1 (NKJV)
- "The angel of the Lord encamps all around those who fear Him and delivers them." Psalm 34:7 (NKJV)
- "You shall also decree a thing, and it shall be established for you..." Job 22:28 (NKJV)
-

Prophetic Declarations

1. I decree that I dwell in the secret place of the Most High, and I abide under the shadow of the Almighty where no evil can reach me, in Jesus' name.

2. I decree that the blood of Jesus covers me, my family, and everything connected to me, and no weapon formed against us shall prosper, in Jesus' name.

3. I decree that I am surrounded by angels day and night, and they bear me up in their hands, preserving me from accidents, attacks, and sudden disasters, in Jesus' name.

4. I decree that the Lord is my refuge and fortress, and no evil shall befall me, nor shall any plague come near my dwelling, in Jesus' name.

5. I decree that I walk through danger unharmed, and every plan of violence, kidnapping, robbery, or destruction is cancelled by divine intervention, in Jesus' name.

6. I decree that every monitoring spirit, demonic trap, or hidden agenda of harm is exposed and destroyed before it manifests, in Jesus' name.

7. I decree that no arrow that flies by day or terror that stalks by night can touch me, because I am hidden in Christ and shielded by His power, in Jesus' name.

8. I decree that I am safe in my coming in and going out, and no tragedy shall locate me, my family, or my property, in Jesus' name.

9. I decree that the Lord is my strong tower, and I run into Him and am lifted above the reach of evil, in Jesus' name.

10. I decree that my environment is spiritually sanitized and free from demonic influence, and the presence of God reigns where I live, work, and travel, in Jesus' name.

11. I decree that divine alarms are activated on my behalf, and any movement of darkness around me is arrested and reversed, in Jesus' name.

12. I decree that I will not be at the wrong place at the wrong time, for the Spirit of the Lord orders my steps and protects my path, in Jesus' name.

13. I decree that I am preserved from untimely

death, sudden calamity, or bloodshed, and I shall live long to fulfil my divine purpose, in Jesus' name.

14. I decree that my sleep is peaceful and undisturbed, for I lie down in safety and wake up with strength, protected by the hand of God, in Jesus' name.

15. I decree that every evil plot, spiritual ambush, or satanic surveillance is shut down by fire, and I walk freely in victory, in Jesus' name.

16. I decree that I am untouchable to the enemy, and any curse, charm, or incantation spoken against me returns to the sender sevenfold, in Jesus' name.

17. I decree that God's presence is my shield, His name is my fortress, and His Word is my defence, in Jesus' name.

18. I decree that I will cross every journey safely, fly, drive, or walk under the divine escort of heaven, and no evil shall intercept my path, in Jesus' name.

19. I decree that I am insulated from evil reports, spiritual arrows, and terminal afflictions, and I walk daily in supernatural safety, in Jesus' name.

20. I decree that divine protection surrounds me like a wall of fire, and nothing shall break through to harm or hinder me, in Jesus' name.

CHAPTER 9

Wisdom, Guidance &
Decision-Making

Life is full of choices, some simple, others life-altering. Every decision you make shapes your destiny. That's why divine wisdom and guidance are not optional for a believer, they are essential. When you walk in God's wisdom, you avoid costly mistakes, align with His will, and navigate life with supernatural insight.

God has promised to lead His people. You are not meant to grope in darkness or lean on your limited understanding. Through the Holy Spirit, God desires to speak clearly into your spirit, guiding you in all things, big or small. Prophetic declarations help you align your mind, heart, and spirit with the wisdom of heaven.

As you declare the Word, you invite the spirit of wisdom to rest upon you. You silence confusion and double mindedness. You break the power of distractions and deception. Your words become a compass, steering you toward divine purpose and away from traps.

Declarations in this chapter will cover your decisions, relationships, business moves, and life direction. They will speak clarity into your spirit and release divine counsel. You will begin to think, speak, and act with God's insight, not just logic, but revelation.

You don't need to fear what lies ahead. God knows the end from the beginning. As you decree His wisdom over your life, you will be led into peace, success, and divine timing.

Key Scriptures:

- "If any of you lacks wisdom, let him ask of God... and it will be given to him." James 1:5 (NKJV)
- "Trust in the Lord with all your heart... and He shall direct your paths." Proverbs 3:56 (NKJV)
- "Your ears shall hear a word behind you, saying, 'This is the way, walk in it.'" Isaiah 30:21 (NKJV)
- "You shall also decree a thing, and it shall be established for you." Job 22:28 (NKJV)
-

Prophetic Declarations

1. I decree that the Spirit of wisdom, understanding, counsel, and might rests upon me, and I make sound decisions that align with God's perfect will, in Jesus' name.

2. I decree that I do not lean on my own understanding, but in all my ways I acknowledge the Lord, and He directs my paths with precision, in Jesus' name.

3. I decree that I have divine insight to discern the right path, choose the right relationships, and avoid every trap of error and confusion, in Jesus' name.

4. I decree that the wisdom of God flows through

me daily, enabling me to solve problems, create solutions, and lead with excellence, in Jesus' name.

5. I decree that I hear the voice of the Holy Spirit clearly, and I am led in the way I should go without hesitation, in Jesus' name.

6. I decree that I do not walk in confusion, double-mindedness, or fear, for my steps are ordered by the Lord and established in righteousness, in Jesus' name.

7. I decree that I have the mind of Christ, and I operate with clarity, creativity, and sharp spiritual discernment in every area of life, in Jesus' name.

8. I decree that every plan I make is divinely inspired, and I receive strategies that cause me to prosper in every good work, in Jesus' name.

9. I decree that I do not miss my timing, my season, or my opportunities, for I walk in sync with God's divine calendar, in Jesus' name.

10. I decree that when I am faced with difficult choices, I receive supernatural clarity and peace to choose wisely, in Jesus' name.

11. I decree that I reject every form of distraction, deception, or manipulation that seeks to divert me from God's will, in Jesus' name.

12. I decree that I am surrounded by wise counsel, godly mentors, and prophetic voices that confirm and sharpen my decisions, in Jesus' name.

13. I decree that my decisions lead to fruitfulness,

promotion, peace, and impact, and not to regret, loss, or destruction, in Jesus' name.

14. I decree that divine intelligence and excellence rest upon me, and I rise above human limitations and mental blocks, in Jesus' name.

15. I decree that I am not confused or overwhelmed, but I operate with calm confidence, because the Spirit of Truth is at work within me, in Jesus' name.

16. I decree that I choose what is excellent, righteous, and aligned with eternity, and I reject shortcuts, compromise, and ungodly alternatives, in Jesus' name.

17. I decree that my spiritual senses are sharp, and I discern between truth and error, divine timing and fleshly impulse, in Jesus' name.

18. I decree that I make decisions that protect my peace, preserve my purpose, and position me for increase, in Jesus' name.

19. I decree that the Lord instructs me even in the night seasons, and His wisdom flows into my spirit whether awake or asleep, in Jesus' name.

20. I decree that I walk in divine direction, make destiny-altering decisions, and fulfil every divine assignment without confusion or delay, in Jesus' name.

CHAPTER 10

Deliverance & Breakthrough

Deliverance is your spiritual inheritance through Christ. You were not saved to remain in bondage, whether it be spiritual oppression, generational curses, mental torment, or demonic strongholds. Jesus came to set the captives free, and His victory on the cross empowers you to walk in complete freedom.

Breakthrough is the visible manifestation of your deliverance. It is when long-standing battles are won, barriers are shattered, and closed doors burst open. In the spirit realm, your breakthrough is already accomplished, your declarations enforce it into your life.

This chapter equips you with powerful declarations that confront spiritual captivity and usher in divine breakthrough. You will speak forth your release from anything that has held you back, cycles of failure, invisible resistance, demonic oppression, or inherited patterns.

When you decree deliverance, you are not begging, you are enforcing. You are aligning your voice with the voice of heaven. You are commanding every Pharaoh to let you go, every wall of Jericho to fall, and every Red Sea to part.

Your words carry power. As you speak in faith, angels are

dispatched, chains are broken, and divine intervention is activated. These declarations will help you move from delay to divine speed, from frustration to fulfilment, from warfare to wonder. Declare boldly. Your deliverance is not in the future, it is now. Your breakthrough is not a possibility; it is a promise.

Key Scriptures:

- "He has delivered us from the power of darkness and conveyed us into the kingdom of the Son of His love." Colossians 1:13 (NKJV)
- "For the weapons of our warfare are not carnal but mighty in God for pulling down strongholds." 2 Corinthians 10:4 (NKJV)
- "You shall also decree a thing, and it shall be established for you." Job 22:28 (NKJV)
- "It shall come to pass in that day that his burden will be taken away from your shoulder... and the yoke will be destroyed because of the anointing." Isaiah 10:27 (NKJV)
-

Prophetic Declarations

1. I decree that every chain of limitation, bondage, and oppression in my life is shattered by the power of God, and I walk free into my divine destiny, in Jesus' name.
2. I decree that every invisible barrier hindering my progress is broken, and I step into unstoppable advancement by the hand of the

Lord, in Jesus' name.

3. I decree that every evil covenant, curse, or spiritual embargo working against my breakthrough is destroyed by the blood of Jesus, in Jesus' name.

4. I decree that I am delivered from every trap, snare, or pit set by the enemy, and I walk in supernatural escape and elevation, in Jesus' name.

5. I decree that every stubborn problem that has resisted prayer and fasting must now bow to the authority of the name of Jesus, in Jesus' name.

6. I decree that I am no longer delayed, denied, or diverted; I walk in divine acceleration and fulfilment of God's promises, in Jesus' name.

7. I decree that the yoke of generational bondage, repeated cycles, and spiritual harassment is broken permanently over my life, in Jesus' name.

8. I decree that I am loosed from every spiritual cage, prison, or chain, and I arise to walk in liberty, Favor, and open doors, in Jesus' name.

9. I decree that the angels of deliverance are working on my behalf, uprooting obstacles and dismantling strongholds erected against my breakthrough, in Jesus' name.

10. I decree that every power sitting on my blessings is unseated by fire, and I take back everything the enemy has stolen from me, in Jesus' name.

11. I decree that the spirit of delay, frustration, and stagnation is rebuked from my life, and I move forward with divine speed, in Jesus' name.

12. I decree that I am free from the influence of marine spirits, witchcraft, sorcery, and occult powers, none shall rule over me, in Jesus' name.

13. I decree that my dreams are redeemed, my visions are restored, and every spiritual attack launched against me in the night is reversed by fire, in Jesus' name.

14. I decree that I break through every wall of resistance, oppression, and hindrance, and I access new realms of glory and answered prayers, in Jesus' name.

15. I decree that I will not go around in circles or repeat failure; I am delivered from every cycle of defeat and released into cycles of victory, in Jesus' name.

16. I decree that I am free from fear, anxiety, and torment, and I walk in boldness, joy, and the sound mind that Christ has given me, in Jesus' name.

17. I decree that deliverance is manifesting in every area of my life, spiritual, financial, emotional, and relational, and I am completely whole, in Jesus' name.

18. I decree that God arises on my behalf, and every enemy, affliction, or stronghold is scattered and consumed by His fire, in Jesus' name.

19. I decree that the anointing of breakthrough rests upon me, and I break forth on every side with testimonies of divine intervention, in Jesus' name.

20. I decree that my season of captivity is over,

and I enter into a new chapter of freedom, expansion, and divine manifestation, in Jesus' name.

CHAPTER 11

Peace of Mind & Emotional Stability

Peace of mind is one of the most precious gifts God offers His children. In a world filled with anxiety, pressure, and uncertainty, God invites you to enter His rest and live in perfect peace. Emotional stability does not mean you are never challenged, it means you are anchored in God, unshaken by the storms around you.

Jesus promised, "Peace I leave with you, My peace I give to you" (John 14:27). This peace transcends human understanding and guards your heart and mind. When your thoughts align with God's Word and your emotions are surrendered to Him, you walk in supernatural calm even when chaos surrounds you.

Many believers struggle silently with fear, worry, depression, or inner turmoil. But today, you must decree and declare your deliverance. You are not called to be a prisoner of emotional instability. God has given you power, love, and a sound mind (2 Timothy 1:7). Your peace is not circumstantial. it is a spiritual inheritance through Christ.

These declarations will help you reject every lie of the enemy, silence inner chaos, and embrace the peace Jesus purchased for you on the cross. Speak them with faith and authority. As you decree peace, you activate it. As you declare emotional strength, you will begin to walk in it. Let the Word of God rule your mind. Let the peace of Christ dominate your atmosphere. You are not a victim of emotional attacks; you are more than a conqueror.

Key Scriptures:

- "You will keep him in perfect peace, whose mind is stayed on You, because he trusts in You." Isaiah 26:3
- "Peace, I leave with you, My peace I give to you." John 14:27
- "God has not given us a spirit of fear, but of power and of love and of a sound mind." 2 Timothy 1:7
- "You shall also decree a thing, and it shall be established for you." Job 22:28

Prophetic Declarations

1. I decree that the peace of God that surpasses all understanding guards my heart and mind, and no storm of life can shake my inner calm, in Jesus' name.
2. I decree that my mind is stayed on the Lord, and I am kept in perfect peace, free from fear, confusion, and emotional unrest, in Jesus' name.
3. I decree that I cast all my cares, worries, and burdens upon the Lord, and I receive His rest, His assurance, and His comfort, in Jesus' name.

4. I decree that the spirit of anxiety, depression, and torment has no power over me, and I walk in the joy and stability of the Holy Spirit, in Jesus' name.

5. I decree that every voice of fear, accusation, and self-doubt is silenced, and I hear only the voice of truth, comfort, and identity from the Lord, in Jesus' name.

6. I decree that I am emotionally whole, healed from every trauma, heartbreak, and disappointment, and I rise with renewed strength and hope, in Jesus' name.

7. I decree that my thoughts are aligned with the Word of God, and I reject every lie, imagination, and stronghold that exalts itself above His truth, in Jesus' name.

8. I decree that I live free from panic attacks, mood swings, and mental pressure, and I enjoy the stillness and serenity of God's presence, in Jesus' name.

9. I decree that my emotions are balanced, my responses are Spirit-led, and my heart is guarded by divine wisdom and love, in Jesus' name.

10. I decree that I sleep peacefully and wake up refreshed, because the Lord gives His beloved rest and surrounds me with angelic peace, in Jesus' name.

11. I decree that I am delivered from emotional manipulation, toxic relationships, and mental traps, and I walk in clarity and discernment, in Jesus' name.

12. I decree that the oil of joy replaces every garment of heaviness, and I rejoice daily in the Lord who renews my strength, in Jesus' name.

13. I decree that I am free from guilt, shame, and regret, and I walk in the assurance of God's forgiveness, love, and acceptance, in Jesus' name.

14. I decree that no trauma from my past shall define my future, for I am healed, whole, and transformed by the power of God, in Jesus' name.

15. I decree that I have a sound mind, free from mental torment, paranoia, and obsessive thoughts, and I live with clarity and purpose, in Jesus' name.

16. I decree that I respond to life with faith, not fear; with joy, not despair; and with hope, not hopelessness, in Jesus' name.

17. I decree that the Holy Spirit is my Comforter, Counsellor, and Guide, and He continually ministers peace, love, and truth to my soul, in Jesus' name.

18. I decree that I walk in emotional maturity and spiritual insight, and I am not easily offended, shaken, or troubled by circumstances, in Jesus' name.

19. I decree that the Prince of Peace rules in my heart, in my home, and in every decision, I make, and I remain anchored in Him, in Jesus' name.

20. I decree that my mind is renewed daily by the

Word, my heart is anchored in God's promises, and I live a life marked by peace and emotional freedom, in Jesus' name.

CHAPTER 12

Favor, Open Doors & Opportunities

There is a season when God opens doors that no man can shut. In His perfect timing, He aligns people, places, and moments to usher you into new opportunities, divine connections, and breakthrough. When God opens a door, it's not by chance, it's by covenant.

Revelation 3:8 says, "See, I have set before you an open door, and no one can shut it." This is your promise. Whether it's a door of Favor, ministry, employment, marriage, or expansion, God holds the key. But many times, fear, delay, or spiritual opposition tries to block or shut doors meant for you. That's why you must boldly decree and declare your entrance into every door of destiny.

When you declare God's Word over your life, you give heaven permission to act on your behalf.

Declarations create divine access points. Even if men try to disqualify you, God's open door bypasses protocol. Like Joseph, who was raised from prison to palace in a day, the doors God opens are often unexpected and supernatural.

In this chapter, you will speak into existence doors that must open and command those that need to close, doors of confusion, delay, or deception. Your declarations will break cycles of denial and stagnation and usher you into seasons of divine movement.

God has gone before you. He has made the crooked paths straight. As you declare these truths, expect uncommon access, divine Favor, and accelerated promotion. You are stepping into rooms your name has already entered.

Key Scriptures:

- "I have set before you an open door, and no one can shut it." Revelation 3:8
- "He opens and no one shuts and shuts, and no one opens." Isaiah 22:22
- "You shall also decree a thing, and it shall be established for you." Job 22:28

Prophetic Declarations

1. I decree that the Favor of God surrounds me like a shield, and everywhere I go, I am remembered, recognized, and rewarded, in Jesus' name.

2. I decree that supernatural doors are opening before me, doors that no man, system, or force can shut, and I walk boldly into divine opportunities, in Jesus' name.

3. I decree that I am highly favoured by God and man, and my name is being mentioned in places of influence, promotion, and breakthrough, in Jesus' name.

4. I decree that I attract opportunities that align with my calling and destiny, and I will not miss my moment of divine visitation, in Jesus' name.

5. I decree that every door of delay, rejection, and disappointment is closed permanently, and new doors of success, Favor, and increase are now open to me, in Jesus' name.

6. I decree that I walk in divine appointments, and my steps are orchestrated to be at the right place, at the right time, with the right people, in Jesus' name.

7. I decree that Favor accelerates my journey, shortens processes, and places me where effort alone could never take me, in Jesus' name.

8. I decree that I am sought after, preferred, and promoted, not by human effort, but by the unexplainable Favor of God operating over my life, in Jesus' name.

9. I decree that every closed gate is opening supernaturally, and I walk into rooms prepared for me by the hand of God, in Jesus' name.

10. I decree that those who have forgotten me are remembering me now, and doors of restoration, access, and reward are opening wide before me, in Jesus' name.

11. I decree that divine opportunities are locating me, and I have the wisdom to discern and embrace them without fear or hesitation, in Jesus' name.

12. I decree that systems, policies, and people are aligning to Favor me, and everything is working together for my elevation, in Jesus' name.

13. I decree that unusual Favor, extravagant blessings, and unexpected breakthroughs are

finding me, overtaking me, and settling in my life, in Jesus' name.

14. I decree that I walk in perpetual Favor, where others are disqualified, I am chosen, and where others are ignored, I am elevated, in Jesus' name.

15. I decree that the Favor of God distinguishes me in every environment, academically, professionally, spiritually, and socially, in Jesus' name.

16. I decree that opportunities that were lost, delayed, or stolen are now restored to me sevenfold by divine justice, in Jesus' name.

17. I decree that I am a carrier of kingdom influence, and doors open not only for me but because of me, as I carry the presence of God, in Jesus' name.

18. I decree that my gifts are making room for me before kings, and I operate in excellence that attracts high places and divine platforms, in Jesus' name.

19. I decree that the season of closed doors and blocked access is over, and I step into a season of open heavens and overflowing blessings, in Jesus' name.

20. I decree that the oil of Favor marks my forehead, and I walk in undeniable grace, continual access, and divine opportunities daily, in Jesus' name.

CHAPTER 13

Purpose, Calling & Ministry

You were not born by accident, you were born on purpose and for a purpose. God designed you with divine intent, and within you is a unique assignment that only you can fulfil. Discovering and walking in your calling is one of the most powerful journeys you can take as a believer.

Jeremiah 1:5 says, "Before I formed you in the womb I knew you; before you were born, I sanctified you; I ordained you a prophet to the nations." Your purpose predates your birth. You were set apart for impact, whether in ministry, business, family, or leadership. The enemy's agenda is to confuse or delay this purpose, but through prophetic declaration, you can unlock clarity, direction, and divine empowerment.

When you decree and declare God's purpose over your life, you align your voice with heaven's assignment. You silence the voices of doubt, fear, and disqualification. Just like David, who moved from the sheepfold to the throne, your journey is guided by divine appointment, not human opinion. Even if you've made mistakes or faced rejection, God's call is irrevocable (Romans 11:29).

This chapter empowers you to boldly decree and declare your divine calling. These declarations will activate clarity, ignite boldness, and silence the voice of comparison. You are not called to be a copy; you are God's original design.

Step out in faith. Embrace your assignment. Let the fire of your calling be rekindled as you release prophetic decrees that commission you for impact.

Key Scriptures:

- "Before I formed you in the womb, I knew you..." Jeremiah 1:5
- "The gifts and the calling of God are irrevocable." Romans 11:29
- "You shall also decree a thing, and it shall be established for you." Job 22:28

Prophetic Declarations

1. I decree that I am chosen, called, and appointed by God to fulfil a divine purpose, and I will not be distracted, delayed, or derailed from my assignment, in Jesus' name.

2. I decree that I walk boldly in the calling of God over my life, and I fulfil it with clarity, power, and excellence, in Jesus' name.

3. I decree that my life is aligned with heaven's blueprint, and I accomplish every task, assignment, and destiny moment ordained for me before time began, in Jesus' name.

4. I decree that every gift and anointing placed in me by God is stirred, refined, and released for His glory and the edification of others, in Jesus' name.

5. I decree that I am a faithful steward of the

ministry God has entrusted to me, and I walk in humility, obedience, and power as I serve His people, in Jesus' name.

6. I decree that I am not called to impress but to impact, and I embrace my unique calling without comparison, competition, or compromise, in Jesus' name.

7. I decree that I have the boldness to say yes to God, the endurance to finish well, and the grace to thrive in every season of my assignment, in Jesus' name.

8. I decree that my voice, my gifts, and my message carry weight in the Spirit, and I am anointed to shift atmospheres and deliver captives, in Jesus' name.

9. I decree that every hindrance, fear, or limitation that has stood against my calling is dismantled, and I rise as a vessel of honour, in Jesus' name.

10. I decree that I will not bury my talent, hide my gift, or abort my assignment; I am fruitful, effective, and courageous in ministry, in Jesus' name.

11. I decree that the fire of God burns in my spirit for His will, and I am not weary in well-doing, for I reap in due season, in Jesus' name.

12. I decree that I have divine helpers, kingdom connections, and strategic partnerships to support and advance the mission of God on my life, in Jesus' name.

13. I decree that my ministry is not built by man but by God, and it carries heaven's endorsement, power, and provision, in Jesus' name.

14. I decree that I am sensitive to the Holy Spirit, moving only when He leads and speaking only what He says, for I am led by Him in all things, in Jesus' name.

15. I decree that I am not a casualty of spiritual warfare, burnout, or compromise, for I dwell in the presence of God and draw strength from Him daily, in Jesus' name.

16. I decree that souls are saved, lives are changed, and God is glorified through my life, and I bear eternal fruit that remains, in Jesus' name.

17. I decree that I am a faithful servant, not seeking titles or applause, but faithfully obeying the One who called me, in Jesus' name.

18. I decree that my legacy is rooted in purpose, and generations after me will rise and follow Christ because of the life I lived, in Jesus' name.

19. I decree that every platform I step on, every message I release, and every assignment I undertake is drenched in grace, truth, and fire, in Jesus' name.

20. I decree that I finish my course with joy, fulfil my calling without apology, and hear the words, "Well done, good and faithful servant," in Jesus' name.

CHAPTER 14

Restoration & New Beginnings

God is a Master Restorer. No matter what has been lost, stolen, or broken in your life, He has the power and desire to restore it beyond its former state. Your past does not have the final word, God does. He specializes in new beginnings and can turn every setback into a setup for glory.

Joel 2:25 declares, "So I will restore to you the years that the swarming locust has eaten..." This is not a mere recovery of possessions or time; it is the redemptive power of God that renews joy, strength, peace, relationships, dreams, and opportunities. When God restores, He multiplies. What seemed like a season of ruin can become a testimony of revival.

There are times when life leaves us feeling as though it's too late to start over, too much has been lost, or we've made too many mistakes. But Isaiah 43:19 reminds us: "Behold, I will do a new thing, now it shall spring forth; shall you not know it?" God is never out of options, and He is not finished with your story.

Decree and declare boldly that your season of restoration and divine reset has come. Speak life to what looks barren. Speak new beginnings over areas that seem dead.

As you release these prophetic declarations, heaven will respond, and the God who makes all things new will begin a new chapter in your life.

Let hope to arise again. Let faith be rekindled. Your latter shall be greater than your former.

Key Scriptures:

- "So, I will restore to you the years..." Joel 2:25
- "Behold, I will do a new thing..." Isaiah 43:19
- "You shall also decree a thing, and it shall be established for you." Job 22:28

Prophetic Declarations

1. I decree that everything lost, stolen, or broken in my life is being divinely restored, and I recover all with interest, in Jesus' name.

2. I decree that my season of dryness, delay, and despair is over, and I step into a new beginning filled with joy, Favor, and forward movement, in Jesus' name.

3. I decree that the God of restoration is breathing life into every dead place in my destiny, and what seemed impossible is now possible by His power, in Jesus' name.

4. I decree that relationships, opportunities, and blessings that were sabotaged or delayed are being restored by the mercy and grace of God, in Jesus' name.

5. I decree that every closed chapter that was meant for my growth is now behind me, and I

walk confidently into a future of purpose and peace, in Jesus' name.

6. I decree that I will not mourn forever over what was lost, because what is coming is greater than what has been, in Jesus' name.

7. I decree that divine restoration touches my health, finances, relationships, reputation, and spiritual fire, and I rise stronger than ever, in Jesus' name.

8. I decree that beauty comes from my ashes, strength replaces my weakness, and joy overwhelms my sorrow, in Jesus' name.

9. I decree that God is rewriting my story, turning my mourning into dancing and giving me a testimony that will silence every accuser, in Jesus' name.

10. I decree that I embrace every divine reset, and I trust that God's plan for my new beginning is filled with hope, increase, and purpose, in Jesus' name.

11. I decree that I will not live in regret or be paralyzed by my past, for God is doing a new thing and it shall spring forth now, in Jesus' name.

12. I decree that I walk into new doors of opportunity, relationships, assignments, and blessings that are perfectly timed by God, in Jesus' name.

13. I decree that every mistake, misstep, or missed season is being redeemed by the blood of Jesus, and my latter days will be greater than the former, in Jesus' name.

14. I decree that what the enemy meant for evil is turning around for my good, and I emerge from every battle with double honour, in Jesus' name.

15. I decree that I am not stuck, stagnant, or sidelined, I am divinely positioned for restoration and elevation, in Jesus' name.

16. I decree that my mind is renewed, my heart is healed, and I embrace the future with faith, courage, and great expectation, in Jesus' name.

17. I decree that new chapters of love, peace, growth, and Favor are opening in my life, and I will not look back, in Jesus' name.

18. I decree that divine surprises, sudden breakthroughs, and unexpected blessings are locating me now, and my restoration is undeniable, in Jesus' name.

19. I decree that I forget the former things and embrace the new, for God is making a way in the wilderness and rivers in the desert for me, in Jesus' name.

20. I decree that this is my season of total restoration, fresh beginnings, and uncommon testimonies that will glorify God, in Jesus' name.

CHAPTER 15

Joy, Hope & Encouragement

Life's battles can drain your strength, cloud your perspective, and steal your joy. But God never intended for His children to walk through life weighed down by despair. In Christ, you have access to supernatural joy that is not based on circumstances, but on His unchanging presence and promises.

Nehemiah 8:10 reminds us that "the joy of the Lord is your strength." Joy is not optional for the believer, it is essential. It fuels your resilience, lifts your spirit, and gives you courage to keep moving forward when everything seems against you. Even in the valley, you can decree and declare joy and hope because God is with you.

Hope anchors your soul (Hebrews 6:19). It is the confident expectation that God is working all things together for your good, even when you cannot see it. Hope is what keeps your prayers alive, your faith active, and your declarations powerful. Romans 15:13 says, "Now may the God of hope fill you with all joy and peace in believing…"

As you speak forth these prophetic declarations, you are choosing to reject sorrow, fear, and discouragement. You are aligning your spirit with the joy and hope that comes from heaven. Declare boldly that your season of heaviness is over and that a garment of praise is your portion.

Encourage yourself in the Lord, as David did (1 Samuel 30:6). Speak light into your darkness and strength into your weariness. Joy is rising. Hope is stirring. A new day is dawning.

Key Scriptures:

- "The joy of the Lord is your strength." Nehemiah 8:10
- "May the God of hope fill you with all joy…" Romans 15:13
- "You shall also decree a thing, and it shall be established for you." Job 22:28

Prophetic Declarations

1. I decree that the joy of the Lord is my strength, and no situation or circumstance can rob me of my divine gladness, in Jesus' name.

2. I decree that hope rises within me today, and I believe again, dream again, and expect again because God is not finished with me, in Jesus' name.

3. I decree that heaviness, sadness, and despair are lifted off me, and I receive the oil of joy and the garment of praise, in Jesus' name.

4. I decree that discouragement has no place in my heart, for my eyes are fixed on the promises of God, and my soul is anchored in His faithfulness, in Jesus' name.

5. I decree that I overflow with joy unspeakable and full of glory, and this joy empowers me to press forward with strength and confidence, in Jesus' name.

6. I decree that every spirit of sorrow, depression, and emotional fatigue is broken off my life, and I rise with supernatural encouragement and inner peace, in Jesus' name.

7. I decree that I am encouraged in the Lord my God, and His Word speaks life, healing, and restoration to every weary place within me, in Jesus' name.

8. I decree that joy is my portion, hope is my posture, and gratitude is my attitude, regardless of what surrounds me, in Jesus' name.

9. I decree that God is turning my mourning into dancing, and my tears are being exchanged for testimonies of praise, in Jesus' name.

10. I decree that I receive good news, divine encouragement, and heavenly reminders of God's promises that lift my spirit, in Jesus' name.

11. I decree that laughter returns to my mouth and songs of joy to my heart, for the Lord has done and is doing great things for me, in Jesus' name.

12. I decree that I do not dwell on the pain of the past, for my future is bright, blessed, and blooming with purpose and peace, in Jesus' name.

13. I decree that I am surrounded by people who uplift, support, and encourage me in the will of God, and every voice of negativity is silenced, in

Jesus' name.

14. I decree that even in waiting, I will rejoice, even in testing, I will trust, and even in hardship, I will worship, in Jesus' name.

15. I decree that I have a heart full of hope, hands lifted in faith, and eyes that see the goodness of the Lord in the land of the living, in Jesus' name.

16. I decree that my soul is revived, my spirit is refreshed, and my heart is restored with the comfort of the Holy Spirit, in Jesus' name.

17. I decree that I will not faint, quit, or give up, for I am being strengthened with might in my inner man and renewed daily, in Jesus' name.

18. I decree that I arise with joy in the morning, walk in hope through the day, and rest in peace through the night, in Jesus' name.

19. I decree that every day I wake up with new mercies, fresh joy, and divine encouragement that empowers me to thrive, in Jesus' name.

20. I decree that I live a life full of joy, overflowing with hope, and saturated with divine encouragement from the throne of grace, in Jesus' name.

CHAPTER 16

Victory over Enemies
& Evil Altars

As a believer in Christ, you are not fighting for victory, you are fighting from victory. The finished work of Jesus on the cross has already disarmed principalities and powers (Colossians 2:15). Yet many battles still arise from evil altars, demonic conspiracies, and spiritual enemies determined to delay, distract, or destroy your destiny. But take heart, you are more than a conqueror through Christ!

Evil altars are spiritual platforms raised by the enemy to invoke curses, limit progress, or manipulate destinies. These altars may operate through ancestral covenants, occult practices, or demonic sacrifices. But the blood of Jesus speaks louder than any altar. By your declarations, you invoke divine judgment against every satanic resistance and activate angelic intervention in your Favor.

Psalm 18:39 declares, "For You have armed me with strength for the battle; You have subdued under me those who rose up against me." When you decree and declare victory over the enemy, you are standing on the authority of the Word and the power of Jesus' name.

Do not be intimidated by what the enemy is doing. No matter how strong the opposition, God has equipped you with divine weapons to pull down strongholds and silence the voice of the enemy (2 Corinthians 10:4-5). Speak against every evil altar raised against your name, family, health, and future. Declare their destruction and proclaim your freedom.

Victory is your portion. The battle is the Lord's, and the outcome is guaranteed. As you declare, expect supernatural reversals, angelic confrontations, and total triumph.

Key Scriptures:

- "Behold, I give you authority... over all the power of the enemy." Luke 10:19
- "You shall also decree a thing, and it shall be established for you." Job 22:28
- "No weapon formed against you shall prosper..." Isaiah 54:17

Prophetic Declarations

1. I decree that every enemy rising against me in judgment is condemned, and I walk in total victory over all demonic opposition, in Jesus' name.

2. I decree that every evil altar raised to monitor, delay, or destroy my life is scattered by fire and rendered powerless forever, in Jesus' name.

3. I decree that I am covered by the blood of Jesus, and no weapon formed against me shall prosper, for the Lord is my shield and defence, in Jesus'

name.

4. I decree that every wicked plot, conspiracy, or curse against my destiny is exposed and reversed by divine authority, in Jesus' name.

5. I decree that the enemies of my progress fall by their own counsel, and their traps turn back upon them sevenfold, in Jesus' name.

6. I decree that I am not afraid of the arrows that fly by day or the terrors that come by night, for the Lord delivers me from every evil assault, in Jesus' name.

7. I decree that every evil priest, enchanter, or sorcerer speaking against my life is silenced, and their sacrifices are rejected by heaven, in Jesus' name.

8. I decree that every altar calling my name for evil is consumed by the fire of the Holy Ghost, and I am released into my divine inheritance, in Jesus' name.

9. I decree that I am not a victim of ancestral bondage, territorial spirits, or generational curses, I am delivered, empowered, and victorious in Christ, in Jesus' name.

10. I decree that my name, my image, and my voice cannot be used against me in any evil gathering, and every monitoring spirit is blinded and paralyzed, in Jesus' name.

11. I decree that I rise above every demonic limitation, barrier, and manipulation, and I walk freely into my purpose with power and speed, in Jesus' name.

12. I decree that divine vengeance is released against every strongman standing at the gate of my breakthrough, and I possess my promised land, in Jesus' name.

13. I decree that I am a terror to the kingdom of darkness, and no enchantment or divination shall prosper against me or my household, in Jesus' name.

14. I decree that every evil voice from shrines, covens, or ancestral roots speaking defeat over my life is permanently silenced by the blood of Jesus, in Jesus' name.

15. I decree that the fire of the Lord goes before me and consumes every demonic obstacle, clearing my path for divine manifestation, in Jesus' name.

16. I decree that I trample upon serpents and scorpions, and nothing shall by any means harm me, for I am clothed in divine authority, in Jesus' name.

17. I decree that my enemies are confused, scattered, and defeated, and the Lord fights my battles while I hold my peace, in Jesus' name.

18. I decree that every altar erected in the realm of darkness to stop my destiny is dismantled, and I rise as a living altar of worship to the Lord, in Jesus' name.

19. I decree that no evil network, alliance, or demonic coalition shall stand against me, for the Lord is with me like a mighty warrior, in Jesus' name.

20. I decree that my victory is permanent, my deliverance is complete, and my enemies are under my feet, never to rise again, in Jesus' name.

CHAPTER 17

Deliverance from
Witchcraft & Sorcery

Witchcraft and sorcery are real spiritual forces that operate to manipulate, control, and destroy lives through demonic power. Many people today suffer battles that defy natural explanation, recurring sicknesses, strange delays, mental oppression, financial ruin, and broken relationships, because of hidden witchcraft operations. But the power of Jesus Christ is greater than all the forces of darkness.

The Bible is clear: "Suffer not a witch to live" (Exodus 22:18, KJV). This is not a call for physical violence but a spiritual charge to dismantle and nullify every spell, curse, or enchantment through fervent prayer and prophetic declarations. As a child of God, you are not a victim, you are a victor! You have been given power to "trample on serpents and scorpions" (Luke 10:19), and no witchcraft shall prevail over you.

Many altars of witchcraft operate through dreams, familiar spirits, occult dedications, or ancestral covenants. But the blood of Jesus cancels every satanic transaction. As you decree and declare your deliverance from witchcraft and sorcery, you enforce your freedom and break the enemy's legal rights over your life.

Decree and declare: Every spell is reversed! Every evil covenant is broken! Every charm is destroyed! Witchcraft chains are falling off now! The fire of the Holy Ghost consumes every agent of darkness assigned against your destiny.

Declare your mind, body, finances, and family off-limits to sorcery and demonic interference. You belong to Jesus, and no enchantment or divination shall succeed against you (Numbers 23:23).

Key Scriptures:

- "There is no sorcery against Jacob, nor any divination against Israel." Numbers 23:23
- "You shall also decree a thing, and it shall be established for you." Job 22:28
- "No weapon formed against you shall prosper..." Isaiah 54:17

Prophetic Declarations

1. I decree that every witchcraft assignment fashioned against my life is destroyed by the fire of God, and I am released into divine liberty, in Jesus' name.

2. I decree that I am hidden under the shadow of the Almighty, and no spell, hex, or incantation can prosper against me or my household, in Jesus' name.

3. I decree that every sorcery or divination summoned to block my progress is overturned by the blood of Jesus, and I break free from every

manipulation, in Jesus' name.

4. I decree that I am delivered from every enchantment, charm, or demonic ritual designed to control or afflict me, in Jesus' name.

5. I decree that every altar of witchcraft raised to monitor, delay, or harm me is scattered by divine thunder, and I escape like a bird from the snare, in Jesus' name.

6. I decree that every witch, warlock, or agent of darkness invoking my name for evil is met with angelic resistance, and their powers are rendered null and void, in Jesus' name.

7. I decree that I am surrounded by the fire of the Holy Ghost, and no demonic force can access or manipulate my life, in Jesus' name.

8. I decree that every form of astral projection, soul travel, or spirit visitation sent against me is arrested and consumed by God's consuming fire, in Jesus' name.

9. I decree that the spirit of witchcraft operating in my environment, family, or community loses its influence over my life and destiny, in Jesus' name.

10. I decree that any food, gift, or contact used as a point of witchcraft access is neutralized by the power in the blood of Jesus, in Jesus' name.

11. I decree that I break out from every spiritual cage of witchcraft confinement, and I rise to walk in my divine purpose, in Jesus' name.

12. I decree that every spell or curse spoken against me is reversed and turned into a blessing by the

hand of the Lord, in Jesus' name.

13. I decree that my dreams, visions, and divine senses are purified and shielded from every form of spiritual interference, in Jesus' name.

14. I decree that I am untouchable by witchcraft powers; I am marked by God's glory and covered by divine fire, in Jesus' name.

15. I decree that every object, token, or item bearing my identity in the witchcraft realm is destroyed by fire, and I reclaim every stolen virtue, in Jesus' name.

16. I decree that every household witchcraft practice affecting my destiny is exposed, uprooted, and judged by the power of the Lord, in Jesus' name.

17. I decree that I rise as a spiritual warrior, empowered by the Holy Spirit to confront and overcome every force of witchcraft, in Jesus' name.

18. I decree that every hidden witchcraft operation working against my health, finances, and family is uncovered and demolished by the fire of the Most High, in Jesus' name.

19. I decree that no evil pronouncement or satanic handwriting shall prevail over my life, for I am delivered from the power of darkness and translated into the Kingdom of light, in Jesus' name.

20. I decree that I live in complete freedom, protected, preserved, and victorious over every witchcraft activity, now and forevermore, in Jesus' name.

CHAPTER 18

Divine Direction & Purpose

One of the greatest needs in a believer's life is divine direction. Without God's guidance, even the best plans can lead to frustration, delay, or destruction. But with divine direction, your life aligns with God's will, and your steps are ordered into fruitfulness, Favor, and fulfilment.

The Bible says in Psalm 37:23 (NKJV): "The steps of a good man are ordered by the Lord, and He delights in his way." God is eager to lead you into your purpose, but you must listen, yield, and obey. He speaks through His Word, through dreams, inner promptings, prophetic insight, and godly counsel. His voice brings peace, clarity, and progress.

Many destinies are trapped in confusion because of wrong decisions, missed instructions, or lack of spiritual discernment. But as you decree and declare divine direction, the veil will lift, confusion will flee, and the light of God will shine on your path. Proverbs 3:56 tells us to trust in the Lord with all our heart and lean not on our own understanding; in all our ways we should acknowledge Him, and He will direct our paths.

Decree and declare that your ears are open, your heart is sensitive, and your feet are moving in sync with heaven's plan. You will not walk in error. You will not waste your time, energy, or resources. You are led by the Spirit of God, and you will fulfil your divine assignment.

Purpose is not something you invent; it is something you discover through divine revelation. As you declare the Word, may every fog of confusion lift, and may divine clarity flood your soul.

Key Scriptures:

- "You shall hear a word behind you, saying, 'This is the way, walk in it.'" Isaiah 30:21
- "The steps of a good man are ordered by the Lord." Psalm 37:23
- "You shall also decree a thing, and it shall be established for you." Job 22:28

Prophetic Declarations

1. I decree that my steps are ordered by the Lord, and I will not walk in confusion or misdirection, for divine clarity rests upon my path, in Jesus' name.

2. I decree that I receive wisdom from above to make decisions that align with God's perfect will and purpose for my life, in Jesus' name.

3. I decree that I am led daily by the Holy Spirit, and I walk confidently into every place God has prepared for me, in Jesus' name.

4. I decree that every veil of confusion, distraction, and deception is removed from my mind, and I receive divine insight to walk in purpose, in Jesus' name.

5. I decree that I do not miss divine appointments, connections, or seasons, for I am in sync with God's timing and direction, in Jesus' name.

6. I decree that I have the mind of Christ, and I discern clearly between the voice of God and every counterfeit or fleshly voice, in Jesus' name.

7. I decree that the light of God shines on my path, exposing every hidden danger and illuminating the way forward with divine precision, in Jesus' name.

8. I decree that I am not derailed by the opinions of men or the pressure of circumstances, but I follow God's leading with boldness and faith, in Jesus' name.

9. I decree that every wrong turn, wasted season, or delay is divinely redeemed, and my journey is accelerated by the grace of God, in Jesus' name.

10. I decree that I walk through open doors of divine assignment, and I reject every counterfeit opportunity meant to derail my destiny, in Jesus' name.

11. I decree that I will fulfil my God-given purpose on earth with accuracy, boldness, and obedience, in Jesus' name.

12. I decree that the fire of God consumes every distraction or detour trying to take me away from my ordained path, in Jesus' name.

13. I decree that my ears are tuned to the frequency of heaven, and I hear the voice of God saying, "This is the way, walk in it," in Jesus' name.

14. I decree that I receive fresh direction, renewed

vision, and divine strategies for every area of my life, in Jesus' name.

15. I decree that divine alignment is my portion, and I am connected to people, places, and platforms that advance my destiny, in Jesus' name.

16. I decree that the fear of the Lord guides my decisions, and I walk in godly wisdom that brings honour, success, and peace, in Jesus' name.

17. I decree that every confusion planted by the enemy in my mind is uprooted, and the peace of God rules my heart and choices, in Jesus' name.

18. I decree that I fulfil heaven's blueprint for my life, and I shall not die with my potential buried, in Jesus' name.

19. I decree that divine purpose unfolds before me daily, and I wake up each day with renewed clarity and excitement to pursue it, in Jesus' name.

20. I decree that I walk in confidence, vision, and fulfilment, knowing that God is leading, empowering, and establishing my every step, in Jesus' name.

CHAPTER 19

Ministry & Spiritual Gifts

Every believer is called to serve in God's Kingdom. Whether on a pulpit or in the marketplace, in the choir or behind the scenes, ministry is not reserved for a select few, it is the duty and privilege of every child of God. And with that calling comes spiritual gifts, divine abilities given by the Holy Spirit to empower us to serve effectively.

1 Peter 4:10 (NKJV) says, "As each one has received a gift, minister it to one another, as good stewards of the manifold grace of God." You have been gifted for impact. Your spiritual gifts are not random; they are strategic, meant to bring glory to God and edification to His people.

Too many believers live unaware of their calling or afraid to step out. But the time to arise is now. As you decree and declare, spiritual gifts will be activated, boldness will be released, and clarity for your ministry will come. You were born for such a time as this. Heaven is waiting for your obedience, and lives are connected to your yes.

Romans 11:29 reminds us that "the gifts and the calling of God are irrevocable." What God has put in you cannot be erased by fear, delay, or rejection. Through prophetic declaration, you stir the gifts, align with heaven, and open doors to ministry assignments divinely prepared for you.

Ministry is not just a role; it's a response to the love of God. Your gift will make room for you (Proverbs 18:16), and your obedience will bear eternal fruit. So, rise up, decree boldly, and step into your anointing.

Key Scriptures:

- 1 Peter 4:10 "Minister it to one another..."
- Romans 11:29 "The gifts and the calling of God are irrevocable."
- Job 22:28 "You shall also decree a thing, and it shall be established for you.

Prophetic Declarations

1. I decree that I am anointed and appointed by God to serve in His Kingdom, and my ministry shall bear fruit that remains, in Jesus' name.

2. I decree that every spiritual gift within me is stirred up, activated, and fully functional to edify the Body of Christ and glorify the Lord, in Jesus' name.

3. I decree that I am a vessel of honour, sanctified and set apart for the Master's use in this generation, in Jesus' name.

4. I decree that no fear, insecurity, or opposition can hinder the flow of the anointing in my life, for the Spirit of the Lord is upon me, in Jesus' name.

5. I decree that I minister with wisdom, grace, and

boldness, and the words of my mouth carry life, healing, and power, in Jesus' name.

6. I decree that the gifts of the Spirit, including prophecy, healing, discernment, wisdom, and tongues, operate freely and effectively in my life, in Jesus' name.

7. I decree that I walk in the fullness of my calling, and I will not be distracted, derailed, or disqualified, in Jesus' name.

8. I decree that I am led by the Holy Spirit in every area of ministry, and I do nothing out of self but through divine instruction, in Jesus' name.

9. I decree that my hands are blessed for Kingdom impact, and miracles, signs, and wonders follow my ministry, in Jesus' name.

10. I decree that I am not intimidated by opposition, for greater is He who is in me than he who is in the world, in Jesus' name.

11. I decree that every spiritual gift God has given me will be used to its fullest potential to bring deliverance, transformation, and revival, in Jesus' name.

12. I decree that I receive supernatural strength, endurance, and wisdom to fulfil my divine assignment without burnout or frustration, in Jesus' name.

13. I decree that I am surrounded by the right spiritual mentors, partners, and covenant helpers who align with God's vision for my life, in Jesus' name.

14. I decree that I am bold as a lion in proclaiming

the gospel, and I do not compromise the truth of God's Word, in Jesus' name.

15. I decree that every resistance to my ministry is broken, and I advance with the fire of God consuming every opposition, in Jesus' name.

16. I decree that my ministry is marked by the presence, power, and purity of God, and many will encounter Jesus through my obedience, in Jesus' name.

17. I decree that I will not bury my talent or sit in silence; I arise and shine as a messenger of hope and healing, in Jesus' name.

18. I decree that doors of nations, platforms, and divine connections open for me to minister, and I walk through them with Favor, in Jesus' name.

19. I decree that I am a faithful steward of God's grace, and I multiply every gift entrusted to me for His glory, in Jesus' name.

20. I decree that my legacy in ministry will echo through generations, and I will hear, "Well done, good and faithful servant," in Jesus' name.

CHAPTER 20

Finances & Provision

God is not only your Healer and Deliverer; He is your Provider. The same God who fed Elijah by ravens, supplied manna to Israel in the wilderness, and filled the widow's jars with oil is still providing for His children today. Financial provision is part of God's covenant with you, and you are not called to a life of lack or endless struggle. Philippians 4:19 (NKJV) declares, "And my God shall supply all your need according to His riches in glory by Christ Jesus." Heaven's economy is never in crisis. While the world may be shaken by inflation, recession, or economic uncertainty, those who trust in the Lord are never forsaken.

God gives you power to get wealth (Deuteronomy 8:18). That means your finances are not just about survival, they're about Kingdom purpose. You are blessed to be a blessing. Every financial declaration you make aligns your life with supernatural abundance, divine Favor, and open doors of provision.

It is time to decree and declare over your finances. Break the grip of lack, command debts to be cancelled, and speak abundance into your business, job, and family.

Faith-filled declarations create financial shifts because your words carry spiritual authority.

As you speak, expect God to release divine ideas, unexpected Favor, and provision from unlikely places. Psalm 23:1 assures us, "The Lord is my shepherd; I shall not want." That is your portion.

Your breakthrough is in your mouth. Open it wide and declare God's provision. The heavens respond when faith speaks.

Key Scriptures:

- Philippians 4:19 "God shall supply all your need..."
- Deuteronomy 8:18 "He gives you power to get wealth."
- Psalm 23:1 "The Lord is my shepherd; I shall not want."
- Job 22:28 "You shall also decree a thing..."

Prophetic Declarations

1. I decree that I walk in supernatural abundance, and every financial struggle in my life is replaced by divine overflow, in Jesus' name.

2. I decree that I am a covenant child of God, and I prosper in all things, even as my soul prospers, in Jesus' name.

3. I decree that my hands are blessed to produce wealth, and I operate in divine ideas, strategies, and opportunities that bring increase, in Jesus' name.

4. I decree that every financial limitation, debt, or burden is broken off my life by the anointing, and I walk in freedom, in Jesus' name.

5. I decree that the heavens are open over my life, and I live under continuous showers of blessings and divine provision, in Jesus' name.

6. I decree that I am not a beggar but a lender to nations, and I live in the overflow of God's goodness and generosity, in Jesus' name.

7. I decree that every seed I sow multiplies exceedingly, and I reap a bountiful harvest in due season without delay, in Jesus' name.

8. I decree that lack and scarcity are far from me, and I enjoy the riches of God's kingdom without sorrow, in Jesus' name.

9. I decree that wealth and riches are in my house, and I use my resources to advance the gospel and bless generations, in Jesus' name.

10. I decree that I am wise in managing my finances, and I walk in discernment, avoiding every trap of waste and financial bondage, in Jesus' name.

11. I decree that God is raising helpers, sponsors, and divine connections to support every vision He has given me, in Jesus' name.

12. I decree that I am not limited by the economy of this world, for my supply comes from the limitless resources of heaven, in Jesus' name.

13. I decree that every delay in financial breakthrough is broken now, and I step into sudden and surprising increase, in Jesus' name.

14. I decree that every curse of poverty, ancestral

debt, or financial stagnation is broken from my life and lineage, in Jesus' name.

15. I decree that I prosper in my business, career, and investments, and my name is associated with excellence and integrity, in Jesus' name.

16. I decree that I will never lack what is needed to fulfil my assignment, raise my family, and bless others, in Jesus' name.

17. I decree that I attract divine Favor for financial opportunities, grants, contracts, and open doors that no man can shut, in Jesus' name.

18. I decree that money serves me and does not control me, and I am a faithful steward of God's provision, in Jesus' name.

19. I decree that I leave an inheritance for my children's children, and my financial legacy will testify of God's faithfulness, in Jesus' name.

20. I decree that my life is a testimony of divine provision, supernatural debt cancellation, and unstoppable prosperity, in Jesus' name.

CHAPTER 21

Destiny Fulfilment & Acceleration

You were not created to drift aimlessly through life. God has a divine purpose, plan, and destiny for you. Before you were formed in your mother's womb, He ordained your life for greatness (Jeremiah 1:5). Destiny is not a random path; it is God's intentional blueprint for your impact on earth.

However, many believers live beneath their calling due to spiritual delays, stagnation, fear, or attacks from the enemy. But the good news is this: your destiny is preserved by God and powered by His Spirit. You can decree and declare your way into fulfilment and divine speed.

Isaiah 60:22 says, "A little one shall become a thousand... I, the Lord, will hasten it in its time." That is divine acceleration. When God steps in, what should take years can happen in moments. Every wasted year can be restored, every missed opportunity redeemed, and every divine appointment realigned.

Decree and declare that your steps are ordered, your path is cleared, and your purpose is unfolding now. No more delays. No more hindrances. You were born for such a time as this, and heaven is backing your advancement.

Declare divine speed over your life, ministry, business, and calling. Break cycles of delay. Command the wind of the Spirit to propel you forward. God is not finished with you; He is just getting started.

Your declarations will unlock divine timing, strategic relationships, and supernatural Favor. As you speak in faith, angels are dispatched, and divine doors are opened.

It's time to run and not be weary, because God is accelerating your destiny.

Key Scriptures:

- Jeremiah 1:5 "Before I formed you... I ordained you."
- Isaiah 60:22 "I, the Lord, will hasten it in its time."
- Habakkuk 2:3 "Though it tarries, wait for it... it will not delay."
- Job 22:28 "You shall also decree a thing..."

Prophetic Declarations

1. I decree that I will not die without fulfilling my divine assignment, and every day of my life moves me closer to my God-ordained purpose, in Jesus' name.

2. I decree that every delay, diversion, and hindrance to my destiny is broken, and I step into supernatural acceleration and fulfilment, in Jesus' name.

3. I decree that I am divinely aligned with people,

places, and opportunities that push me forward into my destiny, in Jesus' name.

4. I decree that my gifts make room for me, and I am brought before kings and influencers who recognize and honour my purpose, in Jesus' name.

5. I decree that I am not behind schedule, for God is redeeming my time and causing everything lost or stolen to be restored sevenfold, in Jesus' name.

6. I decree that every hidden potential and dormant calling within me is awakened, and I rise as a mighty instrument of God's plan, in Jesus' name.

7. I decree that I break out of every generational limitation and step into the fullness of the calling written of me in heaven, in Jesus' name.

8. I decree that I am not distracted or entangled in irrelevant pursuits; I stay focused and faithful to my divine path, in Jesus' name.

9. I decree that no power of hell, human opposition, or personal weakness will abort my destiny, for God's grace sustains and empowers me, in Jesus' name.

10. I decree that I see the big picture and walk with vision, faith, and discipline, embracing every stage of the journey, in Jesus' name.

11. I decree that I move with divine speed and not human effort, and doors that would take years open for me by divine acceleration, in Jesus' name.

12. I decree that I fulfil my divine assignment with joy and effectiveness, leaving a legacy that impacts lives and generations, in Jesus' name.

13. I decree that I overcome every fear, failure, and false start, and I rise stronger, wiser, and more determined to fulfil my calling, in Jesus' name.

14. I decree that I shall not be cut short before my time, and every arrow of untimely death sent to rob my destiny is destroyed, in Jesus' name.

15. I decree that I receive supernatural strength, creativity, and wisdom to carry out every vision, dream, and project God has given me, in Jesus' name.

16. I decree that I run my race with endurance, and I do not compete, compare, or grow weary, for my eyes are fixed on the prize, in Jesus' name.

17. I decree that my name is remembered for good, and the fruit of my labour will speak long after I'm gone, in Jesus' name.

18. I decree that nothing missing, broken, or delayed will define my destiny, but I shall walk in divine wholeness and completion, in Jesus' name.

19. I decree that I will walk through every door assigned to me, and I will not be replaced, removed, or forgotten in my time of purpose, in Jesus' name.

20. I decree that my destiny shall not be delayed, diverted, or destroyed, but it shall manifest in full, for the glory of God, in Jesus' name.

CHAPTER 22

Nations & Global Impact

God is raising voices, vessels, and visionaries in this generation who will not only influence their families or communities but will shake nations and shift global atmospheres. You are called to be a light to the nations; a city set on a hill that cannot be hidden (Matthew 5:14). Your voice, your gifts, your prayers, and your declarations can impact nations for Christ.

God promised Abraham in Genesis 22:18, "In your seed all the nations of the earth shall be blessed." That promise is also yours in Christ Jesus. You are a global influencer, an ambassador of the Kingdom, and a carrier of divine change.

Today's world is filled with unrest, political confusion, wars, and wickedness. Yet, God is not silent. He seeks yielded vessels who will decree His will over nations. Through your prophetic declarations, you can align territories, dismantle demonic altars, and call forth revival.

This chapter encourages you to decree and declare over the nations, your own and others. Speak peace, righteousness, justice, and godly leadership. Break the grip of evil regimes, uproot corruption, and release the gospel with power.

Nations are your inheritance (Psalm 2:8). You were not called to be silent. You are an intercessor, a reformer, and a prophetic voice to the earth. Open your mouth and decree global change.

Declare the Word of the Lord over economies, governments, and generations. Speak life into mission fields, raise altars of worship, and tear down altars of idolatry. The world is waiting for your voice.

Key Scriptures:

- Psalm 2:8 "Ask of Me, and I will give You the nations..."
- Matthew 5:14 "You are the light of the world..."
- Isaiah 60:3 "Gentiles shall come to your light..."
- Job 22:28 "You shall also decree a thing...

Prophetic Declarations

1. I decree that I am a voice to nations, called to bring light, truth, and transformation across borders and territories, in Jesus' name.

2. I decree that doors to the nations open for me without restriction, and I walk through with divine authority and heavenly backing, in Jesus' name.

3. I decree that my words, works, and witness shall influence kings, leaders, and cultures for the glory of God, in Jesus' name.

4. I decree that every limitation trying to confine my impact to one location is broken, and my

reach extends globally by divine mandate, in Jesus' name.

5. I decree that I am a carrier of God's fire and revival, and wherever I go, lives are changed, destinies are awakened, and territories are claimed for Jesus, in Jesus' name.

6. I decree that nations shall call me blessed, and my life will be a conduit of divine help, solutions, and healing to peoples and lands, in Jesus' name.

7. I decree that I have global influence, and my work, message, and ministry spread like wildfire across the earth by the Spirit of God, in Jesus' name.

8. I decree that I am not held back by race, language, nationality, or geography; I rise as a global vessel for Kingdom exploits, in Jesus' name.

9. I decree that embassies, consulates, and borders recognize the Favor of God upon me, and I receive divine access wherever I go, in Jesus' name.

10. I decree that I shall not be rejected, denied, or silenced on the global stage, for my voice is needed and appointed for such a time as this, in Jesus' name.

11. I decree that I walk in uncommon Favor before governments, institutions, and global platforms that elevate Kingdom voices, in Jesus' name.

12. I decree that every demonic resistance from principalities assigned over nations bows to the authority of Christ upon my life, in Jesus' name.

13. I decree that divine provision, translators, connections, and supporters locate me across the globe for the fulfilment of God's assignment, in Jesus' name.

14. I decree that God is raising me as a reformer and ambassador of truth who shapes culture and disciples nations, in Jesus' name.

15. I decree that nations open their treasures to me, and I will not return empty-handed from the land of my assignment, in Jesus' name.

16. I decree that the sound of revival, healing, deliverance, and salvation flows from my life and touches the four corners of the earth, in Jesus' name.

17. I decree that I am hidden from danger and evil while traveling or residing in any part of the world, for the angels of God surround me, in Jesus' name.

18. I decree that the voice of the Lord through me causes nations to bow, reform, and return to righteousness, in Jesus' name.

19. I decree that I shall walk among dignitaries, advise rulers, and release divine counsel that influences policy and societal change, in Jesus' name.

20. I decree that through my life, the glory of the Lord shall cover the earth as the waters cover the sea, in Jesus' name.

CHAPTER 23

Deliverance from Spiritual
Spouse and Marine Kingdom

One of the most hidden but destructive spiritual strongholds affecting destinies today is the operation of spiritual spouses, also known as spirit husbands or spirit wives, and marine kingdom manipulations. These dark powers originate from water-based demonic kingdoms, and they often manifest through dreams of sexual encounters, marital delay, infertility, rejection, and confusion in relationships.

Spiritual spouses are covenant spirits that seek to keep people bound to invisible evil unions, hindering them from enjoying marital harmony, progress, or spiritual growth. Many victims of these powers experience chronic disappointment, failed relationships, miscarriages, and unexplainable emotional or sexual torment. These powers are very real, but the power of Jesus Christ is greater.

In Isaiah 49:24-25, the Lord declares, "Shall the prey be taken from the mighty, or the lawful captive delivered? … I will contend with him who contends with you." You may be a lawful captive due to ancestral covenants or personal involvement (knowingly or unknowingly), but there is deliverance in Christ Jesus. His blood breaks every evil covenant and sets every captive free.

As you decree and declare in this chapter, you are renouncing every demonic marriage and disconnecting from all marine power influences. The declarations are weapons of warfare that dismantle their legal rights and uproot the altars enforcing those covenants.

You are not married to a demon; you are the Bride of Christ. You are not a prisoner of the sea; you are seated with Christ in heavenly places (Ephesians 2:6). As you speak, chains will break, dreams will change, and covenants will be destroyed In Jesus name.

Key Scriptures:

- Isaiah 49:24-25 "Even the captives of the mighty shall be taken away..."
- Hosea 2:2 "Plead with your mother... let her put away her whoredoms..."
- Ephesians 2:6 "Seated with Christ in heavenly places..."
- Job 22:28 "You shall also decree a thing...

Prophetic Declarations

1. I decree that every covenant with spiritual spouses and marine powers is broken by the power in the blood of Jesus, in Jesus' name.

2. I decree that I am loosed from every soul tie, spiritual marriage, or union with spirits from the water kingdom, in Jesus' name.

3. I decree that every demonic ring, garment, or token representing a marine covenant in my life is destroyed by holy fire, in Jesus' name.

4. I decree that every power that visits me in the dream to defile, oppress, or manipulate me is permanently cast out, in Jesus' name.

5. I decree that I am a temple of the Holy Ghost, and no unclean spirit has legal access to my body, mind, or emotions, in Jesus' name.

6. I decree that my spiritual and physical marriage is preserved, protected, and sealed by the blood of Jesus, in Jesus' name.

7. I decree that every evil dedication, initiation, or sacrifice made on my behalf to marine spirits is nullified and rendered powerless, in Jesus' name.

8. I decree that every marine altar speaking against my destiny is silenced forever by the voice of the blood of Jesus, in Jesus' name.

9. I decree that I am released from every spiritual harassment, torment, and oppression associated with water spirits, in Jesus' name.

10. I decree that my children, family, and bloodline are delivered from generational connections to the marine kingdom, in Jesus' name.

11. I decree that my dreams are sanctified, and I no longer experience sexual defilement, manipulation, or covenant renewals in the spirit, in Jesus' name.

12. I decree that every spiritual spouse claiming ownership over my life is permanently divorced by divine judgment, in Jesus' name.

13. I decree that my progress, relationships, and marital destiny are no longer hindered by powers of the sea, in Jesus' name.

14. I decree that every marine power assigned to frustrate, delay, or destroy my destiny is consumed by the fire of God, in Jesus' name.

15. I decree that I am completely disconnected from river, ocean, or ancestral altars of bondage, in Jesus' name.

16. I decree that I live in holiness, righteousness, and purity, and the enemy has no foothold in my life, in Jesus' name.

17. I decree that I recover all that was stolen from me through evil spiritual marriages, my peace, relationships, finances, and Favor, in Jesus' name.

18. I decree that my deliverance is complete, and no marine power can re-enter or re-establish their control over my life, in Jesus' name.

19. I decree that angels of the Lord surround and defend me from every power of seduction and spiritual manipulation, in Jesus' name.

20. I decree that I am fully delivered, divinely restored, and permanently free from every bondage of the marine kingdom, in Jesus' name.

CHAPTER 24

Deliverance from Untimely and Sudden Death

Untimely and sudden death is one of the enemy's most vicious weapons to cut short destinies, end lives prematurely, and steal what God has ordained for His children. The spirit of death often operates through accidents, terminal illnesses, mysterious ailments, tragic occurrences, or spiritual attacks. But Jesus came that you may have life and have it more abundantly (John 10:10).

The enemy may plot death, but God's plan is life. The Bible assures us in Psalm 91:16, "With long life I will satisfy him, and show him My salvation." Long life is a covenant promise for those who dwell in the secret place of the Most High.

Many people live in fear of death because of repeated dreams, evil revelations, or patterns of loss in their families. But as a child of God, you are not to live in fear of sudden destruction. Proverbs 3:25-6 says, "Do not be afraid of sudden terror... for the Lord will be your confidence."

Through these declarations, you will rise to decree and declare your covenant right to life. You will cancel satanic death sentences, overturn graveyard assignments, and speak resurrection over every area of your life. Your voice carries power, and your words release divine protection.

You will not die but live to declare the works of the Lord (Psalm 118:17). The grave will not rejoice over you. Every coffin prepared for your life or family shall catch fire. You are covered by the blood of Jesus, and no evil shall befall you in Jesus name.

Let every fear of death die as you declare with boldness that your life is hidden in Christ!

Key Scriptures:

- Psalm 91:16 "With long life I will satisfy him..."
- John 10:10 "I have come that they may have life..."
- Proverbs 3:25-26 "Do not be afraid of sudden terror..."
- Psalm 118:17 "I shall not die, but live..."
- Job 22:28 "You shall also decree a thing..."
-

Prophetic Declarations

1. I decree that I shall not die prematurely, but I shall live to declare the works of the Lord in the land of the living, in Jesus' name.

2. I decree that every appointment with sudden death is cancelled, and I walk under the covering of divine preservation, in Jesus' name.

3. I decree that the spirit of death has no power over me, for I am hidden in Christ and covered by the blood of Jesus, in Jesus' name.

4. I decree that every arrow of sudden death fired against me, or my loved ones returns to the sender by fire, in Jesus' name.

5. I decree that I and my family will not be victims of road accidents, armed robbery, stray bullets, or natural disasters, in Jesus' name.

6. I decree that no sickness or affliction shall lead to untimely death in my body, for I have the life of God within me, in Jesus' name.

7. I decree that every grave prepared for me, or anyone connected to me shall remain empty, for we shall not be buried before our time, in Jesus' name.

8. I decree that I am delivered from every curse of premature death that runs through my bloodline, in Jesus' name.

9. I decree that my life is preserved from every trap, ambush, and evil plot of the enemy to destroy me suddenly, in Jesus' name.

10. I decree that I shall live to fulfil my divine assignment and not be cut off in the middle of my purpose, in Jesus' name.

11. I decree that no witchcraft spell, occult ritual, or evil sacrifice shall claim my life or that of my loved ones, in Jesus' name.

12. I decree that I am untouchable by the spirit of death, for the Lord is my refuge and my fortress, in Jesus' name.

13. I decree that every evil dream of death is cancelled and shall not manifest, for I am secured by angelic protection, in Jesus' name.

14. I decree that I walk in wisdom, divine timing, and protection, and I shall not be at the wrong place at the wrong time, in Jesus' name.

15. I decree that every obituary issued against my life is torn by fire, and my name shall not be associated with death prematurely, in Jesus' name.

16. I decree that my blood shall not be spilled, and no weapon formed against me shall prosper, in Jesus' name.

17. I decree that I rise above every valley of the shadow of death, and I fear no evil, for God is with me, in Jesus' name.

18. I decree that my home is marked by the blood of Jesus, and the destroyer shall pass over us, in Jesus' name.

19. I decree that my dreams, visions, and goals will not die with me, for I shall live to see them fulfilled, in Jesus' name.

20. I decree that the number of my days I shall fulfil, and I shall go to the grave in peace, not by tragedy or demonic arrangement, in Jesus' name.

CHAPTER 25

Deliverance from Evil Arrows

In the spiritual realm, arrows are symbolic of targeted attacks from the enemy, whether through words, curses, sickness, affliction, setbacks, or sudden calamities. Evil arrows are invisible weapons shot at individuals with the aim of destroying health, peace, finances, marriages, relationships, and destinies. But no weapon formed against you shall prosper (Isaiah 54:17).

The Bible speaks of these arrows in Psalm 91:5: "You shall not be afraid of the terror by night, nor of the arrow that flies by day." This reveals that arrows can fly at any time, day or night. They can manifest as confusion, chronic illness, nightmares, business failure, family conflict, or spiritual heaviness.

However, as a believer, you are not defenceless. God has given you authority through His Word to stop and reverse every evil arrow. By the blood of Jesus and the power of your declarations, you can send those arrows back to the sender. You can decree and declare divine immunity and supernatural escape from every demonic ambush.

Ephesians 6:16 tells us that the shield of faith can quench every fiery dart (or arrow) of the wicked one. You are not a victim; you are a victor. Through the name of

Jesus and prophetic decrees, you can dismantle every evil projection and terminate every satanic assignment launched against you.

These declarations will empower you to rise in spiritual warfare and reclaim your freedom from every satanic arrow. Whether it is an arrow of sickness, madness, poverty, barrenness, or confusion, the Lord will deliver you and restore your peace.

Key Scriptures:

- Psalm 91:5 "Nor of the arrow that flies by day…"
- Isaiah 54:17 "No weapon formed against you shall prosper…"
- Ephesians 6:16 "The shield of faith… quenches all fiery darts…"
- Job 22:28 "You shall also decree a thing, and it shall be established…"

Prophetic Declarations

1. I decree that every evil arrow fired against my life, health, destiny, or family is reversed by fire and returns to its sender, in Jesus' name.

2. I decree that no weapon formed or fashioned against me shall prosper, and every tongue that rises in judgment is condemned, in Jesus' name.

3. I decree that the shield of faith quenches every fiery dart of the enemy targeted at me day or night, in Jesus' name.

4. I decree that I am hidden in the secret place of the Most High, and evil arrows shall not locate

me or those connected to me, in Jesus' name.

5. I decree that arrows of sickness, poverty, confusion, shame, and delay shall not penetrate my life or destiny, in Jesus' name.

6. I decree that every invisible arrow fired at me in the dream or while awake is shattered by the power of God, in Jesus' name.

7. I decree that the blood of Jesus surrounds me as a barrier, and evil shall not befall me or my household, in Jesus' name.

8. I decree that I am immune to spiritual attacks, and my life repels demonic arrows by divine fire, in Jesus' name.

9. I decree that arrows fired against my marriage, career, ministry, or children shall be intercepted by angelic warriors, in Jesus' name.

10. I decree that my spirit, soul, and body are covered by divine Armor, and no demonic projection can harm me, in Jesus' name.

11. I decree that every arrow of sudden disaster, setback, or depression sent to derail me is consumed by the fire of the Holy Ghost, in Jesus' name.

12. I decree that I walk daily in divine immunity, and no enchantment or divination against me shall stand, in Jesus' name.

13. I decree that every arrow programmed into my environment, food, or atmosphere shall be neutralized by the power of God, in Jesus' name.

14. I decree that arrows of fear, doubt, and spiritual dryness shall not prevail against me, for I am

rooted in God, in Jesus' name.

15. I decree that every evil arrow targeting my finances and progress is broken and sent back to the camp of the wicked, in Jesus' name.

16. I decree that my home, workplace, and ministry are fire-zones, and evil cannot dwell or operate there, in Jesus' name.

17. I decree that the arrow of false accusation, betrayal, and conspiracy is silenced and turned into a testimony for my lifting, in Jesus' name.

18. I decree that I escape every trap of the enemy, and no evil arrow shall waste my time, resources, or energy, in Jesus' name.

19. I decree that every evil pronouncement or curse functioning as an arrow is nullified by the blood of the Lamb, in Jesus' name.

20. I decree that I am covered under God's wings, preserved from evil arrows, and victorious in every battle, in Jesus' name.

CHAPTER 26

Deliverance from Monitoring Spirits

Monitoring spirits, also known as familiar spirits or spiritual spies, are demonic agents sent to observe, track, and report the activities of God's children. These spirits aim to delay breakthroughs, cause repetitive cycles of failure, and block divine progress. They are often responsible for strange patterns, rising and falling, and sudden hindrances just before a breakthrough.

In Acts 16:16, Paul and Silas encountered a girl possessed with a spirit of divination. Though she spoke truth, her information came from a demonic source that aimed to subtly disrupt God's work. This is how monitoring spirits operate, masquerading as harmless while gathering intelligence to launch attacks.

These spirits can work through dreams, people, objects, or environments. They may take the form of animals in dreams, such as cats, birds, or snakes, or manifest through individuals who always seem to know your private matters. But as a believer, you have authority in Christ to break free from every demonic surveillance.

Through fervent prayers and prophetic decrees, you can blind the eyes of monitoring spirits, shut their channels, and disconnect yourself from their networks. Declare that your life is hidden with Christ in God (Colossians 3:3), and no weapon of demonic intelligence shall prosper against you.

Decree and declare your freedom. Call forth confusion into their camp. Sever every spiritual tracking device and destroy every evil mirror or altar being used to monitor your life.

You are not a victim, you are covered by the blood and surrounded by fire!

Key Scriptures:

- Acts 16:16 "A certain slave girl possessed with a spirit of divination met us..."
- Colossians 3:3 "For you died, and your life is hidden with Christ in God."
- Isaiah 8:10 "Take counsel together, but it will come to nothing..."
- Job 22:28 "You shall also decree a thing, and it shall be established..."

Prophetic Declarations

1. I decree that every monitoring spirit assigned to observe, report, or hinder my progress is blinded by the fire of God, in Jesus' name.

2. I decree that I am hidden in Christ and covered by the blood of Jesus; no evil eye shall trace or locate me, in Jesus' name.

3. I decree that every demonic mirror, satellite, or spiritual gadget used to track my movements is

shattered into pieces, in Jesus' name.

4. I decree that every agent of darkness spying on my family, ministry, business, or destiny is exposed and disgraced, in Jesus' name.

5. I decree that I escape every trap set through spiritual surveillance, and the enemy shall fall into the pit they dug for me, in Jesus' name.

6. I decree that every familiar spirit assigned to follow me around spiritually or physically is arrested by the angels of the Lord, in Jesus' name.

7. I decree that every human or demonic agent gathering information about me for evil purposes is silenced and rendered powerless, in Jesus' name.

8. I decree that my atmosphere is saturated with the glory of God, and no unclean presence can operate around me, in Jesus' name.

9. I decree that I walk in divine secrecy and security, and no enemy shall predict, manipulate, or sabotage my destiny, in Jesus' name.

10. I decree that every spiritual drone monitoring my dreams, breakthroughs, and movements is shot down by divine arrows, in Jesus' name.

11. I decree that I am no longer visible or accessible to satanic networks, covens, or occult watchers, in Jesus' name.

12. I decree that the Holy Ghost confuses and scatters every demonic intelligence system set up against my life, in Jesus' name.

13. I decree that I receive angelic escorts who protect me from monitoring spirits and demonic informants, in Jesus' name.

14. I decree that every household enemy monitoring me under the guise of friendship or care is exposed and removed from my life, in Jesus' name.

15. I decree that all satanic observers assigned to delay, block, or steal my blessings are blinded and bound forever, in Jesus' name.

16. I decree that the power of monitoring spirits over my dreams, visions, and spiritual gifts is destroyed by the anointing, in Jesus' name.

17. I decree that I am a fire carrier and monitoring spirits cannot stand the intensity of the presence of God in my life, in Jesus' name.

18. I decree that I am completely disconnected from every network of spiritual spies working against me, in Jesus' name.

19. I decree that I am guarded by divine surveillance and heavenly watchers who frustrate the works of darkness on my behalf, in Jesus' name.

20. I decree that every trace of monitoring spirits in my environment, bloodline, or associations is erased and destroyed, in Jesus' name.

CHAPTER 27

Deliverance from Foundational Strongholds

Foundational strongholds are spiritual problems rooted in your family lineage, ancestry, or early life experiences. These are deep-seated issues that have existed for generations, patterns of failure, poverty, sickness, marital delay, barrenness, untimely death, or idolatry, passed down from one generation to another. These strongholds often go unnoticed until their effects begin to show in recurring limitations, strange battles, and stubborn cycles.

Psalm 11:3 declares, "If the foundations are destroyed, what can the righteous do?" This means that even when you are born again, unresolved foundational issues can still wage war against your progress unless they are confronted and broken by the power of God.

Many people are fighting battles they did not start; problems inherited through bloodlines. Just as blessings can flow through a generational covenant, so can curses and bondages. If your foundation was built on witchcraft, idol worship, sexual immorality, broken covenants, or bloodshed, these things can give the enemy legal ground to afflict your destiny.

But there is good news: Jesus came to destroy the works of the devil (1 John 3:8). Through deliverance prayers, prophetic declarations, and renouncing evil foundations, you can rebuild your life on the unshakable Rock, Jesus Christ.

This chapter invites you to rise and decree and declare freedom from every foundational bondage. Speak into your roots and command every evil tree to be uprooted. Declare a new beginning in your bloodline and plant yourself in the truth and power of God's Word.

You will rise from every faulty foundation and fulfil your divine purpose!

Key Scriptures:

- Psalm 11:3 "If the foundations are destroyed, what can the righteous do?"
- Jeremiah 1:10 "To root out and to pull down, to destroy and to throw down..."
- 1 John 3:8 "...For this purpose the Son of God was manifested, that He might destroy the works of the devil."
- Job 22:28 "You shall also decree a thing, and it shall be established..."

Prophetic Declarations

1. I decree that every evil foundation speaking against my destiny is broken and replaced by the unshakable foundation of Christ, in Jesus' name.
2. I decree that every ancestral covenant, vow, or dedication affecting my life negatively is nullified by the power in the blood of Jesus, in

Jesus' name.

3. I decree that I am separated from the foundational limitations, failures, and patterns that afflicted my family line, in Jesus' name.

4. I decree that every voice of foundational altars calling my name for destruction is silenced by divine fire, in Jesus' name.

5. I decree that the strongman assigned to enforce evil cycles in my lineage is bound and cast out forever, in Jesus' name.

6. I decree that I am no longer a prisoner of generational errors, curses, or iniquities; I walk in newness of life, in Jesus' name.

7. I decree that every demonic root anchoring poverty, sickness, marital delay, or spiritual weakness in my life is uprooted now, in Jesus' name.

8. I decree that my bloodline is cleansed by the blood of Jesus, and no demonic inheritance shall prevail against me, in Jesus' name.

9. I decree that every foundational gatekeeper blocking my breakthrough is dethroned by the authority of Christ, in Jesus' name.

10. I decree that I am disconnected from every evil dedication, sacrifice, or ritual performed on my behalf knowingly or unknowingly, in Jesus' name.

11. I decree that the foundational demons that tormented my ancestors shall not have access to my life or generations after me, in Jesus' name.

12. I decree that I walk in freedom from inherited

shame, reproach, and repeated failures, in Jesus' name.

13. I decree that the mercy of God speaks louder than the accusations rising from my family foundation, in Jesus' name.

14. I decree that I escape every ancestral pattern of sudden death, delay, barrenness, or stagnation by divine intervention, in Jesus' name.

15. I decree that my foundation is rebuilt on righteousness, peace, and the covenant of grace, in Jesus' name.

16. I decree that I break out from every spiritual prison connected to my father's or mother's house, in Jesus' name.

17. I decree that I am a new creation; old things tied to my bloodline are passed away, and all things have become new, in Jesus' name.

18. I decree that every altar of affliction erected in my lineage is pulled down and consumed by fire, in Jesus' name.

19. I decree that my testimony shall be different, and my life shall reflect divine exceptions from family bondage, in Jesus' name.

20. I decree that I possess my possessions and rise above every foundational stronghold by the authority of Christ, in Jesus' name.

CHAPTER 28

Deliverance from Curses

A curse is a spiritual sentence or judgment pronounced upon a person, family, or generation that brings hardship, misfortune, stagnation, or destruction. It is the opposite of a blessing. Curses can originate from sin, disobedience, occult involvement, broken covenants, idol worship, or evil pronouncements. Some are self-imposed, others are inherited or transferred through bloodlines.

Deuteronomy 28 outlines both the blessings for obedience and the curses for disobedience. Many people today are suffering not because they are lazy or unskilled, but because unseen curses are working against their progress. These curses can affect finances, health, relationships, and destiny fulfilment.

But thank God for Jesus Christ! Galatians 3:13 boldly declares, "Christ has redeemed us from the curse of the law, having become a curse for us…" Through His sacrifice on the cross, the power of every curse was broken. You are no longer under the dominion of any evil pronouncement or generational bondage.

Still, these curses must be confronted, renounced, and cancelled by faith-filled declarations. As you decree and declare today, you are enforcing your covenant rights in

Christ. You are standing on the legal victory that Jesus secured through His blood. Speak boldly and uproot every curse, spoken or written, nullifying its effect by the power in the name of Jesus.

You are not cursed; you are blessed and highly favoured!

Key Scriptures:

- Galatians 3:13 "Christ has redeemed us from the curse of the law..."
- Proverbs 26:2 "Like a flitting sparrow... so a curse without cause shall not alight."
- Numbers 23:8 "How shall I curse whom God has not cursed?"
- Job 22:28 "You shall also decree a thing, and it shall be established for you..."

Prophetic Declarations

1. I decree that every curse spoken over my life, family, or bloodline, knowingly or unknowingly, is broken by the power in the blood of Jesus, in Jesus' name.

2. I decree that I am redeemed from the curse of the law, and no generational curse has legal right to operate in my life, in Jesus' name.

3. I decree that every word curse, hex, or negative utterance released against me is nullified and rendered powerless, in Jesus' name.

4. I decree that I am no longer subject to cycles of failure, rejection, barrenness, or poverty caused by ancestral or personal curses, in Jesus' name.

5. I decree that the voice of mercy and grace silences every voice of condemnation, judgment, or accusation operating through curses, in Jesus' name.

6. I decree that every self-imposed curse spoken out of ignorance or fear is cancelled and replaced with blessings, in Jesus' name.

7. I decree that I walk under the covering of divine Favor and no enchantment or divination shall prevail against me, in Jesus' name.

8. I decree that every altar empowering curses against my name, progress, or destiny is destroyed by fire, in Jesus' name.

9. I decree that I am disconnected from the curse of delay, stagnation, and fruitlessness; I enter into God's covenant of speed and fruitfulness, in Jesus' name.

10. I decree that the curse of premature death, mental torment, or constant failure is uprooted from my lineage and life, in Jesus' name.

11. I decree that I walk in the blessing of Abraham, and the curses of my father's house shall not determine my future, in Jesus' name.

12. I decree that every curse of marital failure, broken relationships, or loneliness is broken, and I enter into divine settlement, in Jesus' name.

13. I decree that I will not labour under curses but flourish under the covenant of the blood of Jesus, in Jesus' name.

14. I decree that every curse of infirmity, chronic

illness, or inherited disease is terminated, and I receive divine healing, in Jesus' name.

15. I decree that every curse rooted in rebellion, idolatry, or disobedience in my family is reversed and washed away by the blood, in Jesus' name.

16. I decree that I am no longer under the influence of curses released through witchcraft, sorcery, or satanic dedications, in Jesus' name.

17. I decree that I am free from environmental, territorial, and community-based curses, and I walk in the liberty of Christ, in Jesus' name.

18. I decree that the blessings of the Lord make me rich and add no sorrow; no curse shall subtract from my divine inheritance, in Jesus' name.

19. I decree that I am surrounded by the fire of the Holy Spirit, and curses cannot penetrate my covenant covering, in Jesus' name.

20. I decree that I am blessed beyond limits, empowered to prosper, and filled with grace to fulfil destiny without hindrance, in Jesus' name.

CHAPTER 29

Marital Restoration and Healing

Marriage is God's divine institution designed for companionship, covenant love, and the fulfilment of purpose. However, many marriages today are under intense attack, facing separation, emotional disconnection, infidelity, constant conflict, or even divorce. The enemy targets marriages because he knows that strong families build strong destinies and godly legacies.

Whether you are praying for your own marriage, standing in the gap for your spouse, or interceding for a broken union, know this: God is a Restorer.

He can heal what has been wounded and resurrect what looks dead. In Malachi 2:16, the Lord says, "I hate divorce," revealing His desire for covenant reconciliation. He is able to mend hearts, rekindle love, and rebuild trust when we invite Him in.

Ezekiel 37:3 asks, "Son of man, can these bones live?" And the answer is YES! No matter how lifeless your relationship seems, God's power can breathe new life into it. Restoration begins with prayer, humility, and the declaration of God's promises over your marriage. As you decree and declare, heaven will align with your faith to repair, restore, and renew what the enemy tried to destroy.

Let these prophetic declarations uproot bitterness, break ungodly soul ties, restore emotional intimacy, and release the oil of peace in your home. Don't accept turmoil, speak life into your marriage and expect healing.

Key Scriptures:

- Joel 2:25 "I will restore to you the years that the locust has eaten…"
- Ezekiel 37:5 "Surely I will cause breath to enter into you, and you shall live."
- Malachi 2:16 "For the Lord God of Israel says that He hates divorce…"
- Job 22:28 "You shall also decree a thing, and it shall be established for you…"

Prophetic Declarations

1. I decree that every broken wall in my marriage is rebuilt by the hand of the Lord, and divine love and unity are restored between my spouse and me, in Jesus' name.

2. I decree that every root of bitterness, offense, and unforgiveness is uprooted from my heart and my marriage, and replaced with peace and healing, in Jesus' name.

3. I decree that any evil voice speaking division, confusion, or separation into my marriage is silenced by the voice of the Lord, in Jesus' name.

4. I decree that God's original purpose for my

marriage is revived and reestablished in power and joy, in Jesus' name.

5. I decree that the Spirit of humility, patience, and understanding fills our home, and every spirit of strife, competition, or pride is banished, in Jesus' name.

6. I decree that the fire of intimacy, trust, and godly companionship is rekindled in my relationship, and every strange fire is extinguished, in Jesus' name.

7. I decree that no external influence, third-party manipulation, or strange woman/man shall enter or destroy my marriage, in Jesus' name.

8. I decree that my marriage is a testimony of God's covenant faithfulness and is covered by divine protection, in Jesus' name.

9. I decree that every emotional wound caused by betrayal, hurt, or past trauma is healed by the balm of Gilead, in Jesus' name.

10. I decree that I am empowered to love, respect, and honour my spouse as Christ commands, and I receive grace to model kingdom marriage, in Jesus' name.

11. I decree that every manipulation of darkness against my marriage covenant is destroyed, and every attack on our unity is reversed, in Jesus' name.

12. I decree that peace reigns in my home and confusion, tension, and anger lose their grip, in Jesus' name.

13. I decree that my spouse's heart is drawn back to

God and to me, and divine alignment is restored in our relationship, in Jesus' name.

14. I decree that every financial, emotional, or spiritual struggle causing friction in my marriage is replaced with divine provision and agreement, in Jesus' name.

15. I decree that we are united in purpose, mission, and destiny, and every agenda of division is permanently cancelled, in Jesus' name.

16. I decree that godly counsel and wisdom guide our decisions, and foolishness, immaturity, and selfishness are removed from our home, in Jesus' name.

17. I decree that our children (present or future) are blessed, shielded from generational patterns of marital failure, and raised in love and truth, in Jesus' name.

18. I decree that the generational curses of separation, infidelity, or divorce are broken and will not continue through our lineage, in Jesus' name.

19. I decree that my marriage flourishes like a well-watered garden, fruitful in love, faithfulness, purpose, and joy, in Jesus' name.

20. I decree that the blood of Jesus seals and secures our marital covenant, and no weapon formed against it shall prosper, in Jesus' name.

CHAPTER 30

*Divine Acceleration
and Overtaking*

There are seasons when it feels like life has delayed or passed you by. Years may have been lost to sickness, stagnation, poor choices, or spiritual attacks. But the God you serve is not only a Restorer, He is the God of Divine Acceleration. He doesn't just catch you up; He causes you to overtake and gain more than what was lost.

In 1 Kings 18:46, the Bible says, "Then the hand of the Lord came upon Elijah; and he girded up his loins and ran ahead of Ahab to the entrance of Jezreel." Elijah, empowered by the Spirit, outran a chariot! That is acceleration beyond the natural. Divine acceleration means achieving in months what would ordinarily take years, because God Himself removes the delay and drives your progress.

This chapter's prophetic declarations are designed to shift you into divine momentum. As you decree and declare, delay will give way to destiny. Every power of limitation, every spiritual roadblock, and every cycle of slowness will be broken. You will move forward, and you will overtake.

Joel 2:25 assures us that God restores the years stolen by

the enemy. You will not only recover lost time, but you will advance with divine speed. Let your words carry the weight of heaven as you declare God's promises over your life.

It's time to arise and run with purpose. Acceleration is your portion, and overtaking is your testimony.

Key Scriptures:

- 1 Kings 18:46 "The hand of the Lord came upon Elijah... and he ran ahead of Ahab."
- Joel 2:25 "I will restore to you the years that the locust has eaten..."
- Amos 9:13 "The Plowman shall overtake the reaper..."
- Job 22:28 "You shall also decree a thing, and it shall be established for you..."

Prophetic Declarations

1. I decree that every delay in my life is broken, and by divine acceleration, I overtake lost time, missed seasons, and forgotten opportunities, in Jesus' name.
2. I decree that where I have been crawling, I will now soar by the wind of the Spirit, and what should take years will take months by God's supernatural speed, in Jesus' name.
3. I decree that divine help, Favor, and strategic connections locate me urgently to move me forward beyond my current limitations, in Jesus' name.

4. I decree that every power holding back my destiny progress is scattered by the fire of God, and my advancement begins today, in Jesus' name.

5. I decree that my steps are divinely ordered into the right places, right people, and right opportunities that catapult me forward, in Jesus' name.

6. I decree that I will recover all that the enemy stole from me, opportunities, time, relationships, and finances, by divine acceleration, in Jesus' name.

7. I decree that the anointing of Elijah that outran the king's chariot comes upon me to outrun my competitors and every delay, in Jesus' name.

8. I decree that by divine mandate, I break free from slow progress and backwardness and enter my season of unusual speed and elevation, in Jesus' name.

9. I decree that the God of restoration multiplies my results and compresses years of labour into weeks of reward, in Jesus' name.

10. I decree that I will no longer be behind schedule in life; I walk in divine timing and perfect alignment with heaven's calendar, in Jesus' name.

11. I decree that what others struggle for, I receive with ease through divine Favor and accelerated grace, in Jesus' name.

12. I decree that my waiting season turns into a winning season, and everything that was

stagnant begins to move by divine fire, in Jesus' name.

13. I decree that doors that have been shut against me are suddenly opened, and divine access is granted speedily, in Jesus' name.

14. I decree that the angels of acceleration are assigned to my destiny to fast-track my miracles and breakthroughs, in Jesus' name.

15. I decree that my voice is heard, my gifts are seen, and my calling is recognized and rewarded without unnecessary delay, in Jesus' name.

16. I decree that there shall be no more postponement or stagnation in my life; my next level begins now, in Jesus' name.

17. I decree that divine overtaking comes upon me, I overtake those who have gone ahead of me because of divine grace, in Jesus' name.

18. I decree that I am released from every traffic of delay on my destiny path, and I now run with divine speed toward my promises, in Jesus' name.

19. I decree that where I was forgotten or ignored, I am now remembered and accelerated into prominence and purpose, in Jesus' name.

20. I decree that the Spirit of divine speed rests upon me, and I accomplish in one year what others take a lifetime to build, in Jesus' name.

CHAPTER 31

Establishment and Settlement

After the battles, the delays, the wandering, and the waiting, there comes a divine season called settlement. God's will is not for you to be unstable, always shifting, or perpetually fighting to survive. His desire is to establish you, in purpose, in family, in calling, and in every area of your life.

1 Peter 5:10 declares, "But may the God of all grace, who called us to His eternal glory by Christ Jesus, after you have suffered a while, perfect, establish, strengthen, and settle you." This is God's promise to those who have endured: not only restoration, but also permanence, strength, and peace.

To be settled is to be rooted and grounded. It means no more jumping from job to job, no more broken relationships, no more uncertain paths. It means a home, a legacy, and a firm foundation. These declarations are designed to call forth your season of divine settlement.

As you decree and declare these prophetic words, chains of instability will break. You will move from wandering to dwelling, from transition to territory, from frustration to fulfilment. God will plant you in your own land and establish you in His promises.

No more circles. No more unsettled seasons. It's time to dwell in the land and feed on His faithfulness. You will be settled. You will be established.

Key Scriptures:

- 1 Peter 5:10 "...after you have suffered a while, perfect, establish, strengthen, and settle you."
- Psalm 40:2 "He set my feet upon a rock and established my steps."
- Deuteronomy 28:9 "The Lord will establish you as a holy people to Himself..."
- Job 22:28 "You shall also decree a thing, and it shall be established for you...

Prophetic Declarations

1. I decree that I am divinely established in every area of my life, and nothing shall uproot me from the will and purpose of God, in Jesus' name.

2. I decree that the Lord who settles the righteous settles me in peace, prosperity, marriage, ministry, and destiny without delay, in Jesus' name.

3. I decree that I am no longer a wanderer or drifter in life; the hand of the Lord plants me on a solid rock, in Jesus' name.

4. I decree that instability and double mindedness are broken from my life, and I am rooted in divine direction and clarity, in Jesus' name.

5. I decree that I am settled in my rightful place

spiritually, emotionally, relationally, financially, and geographically, according to the divine blueprint, in Jesus' name.

6. I decree that I am no longer a victim of cycles or patterns that displace me from my place of blessing, in Jesus' name.

7. I decree that by the grace of God, I enter into a season of rest and settlement where battles cease and blessings flow, in Jesus' name.

8. I decree that I am no longer tossed to and for by storms, confusion, or spiritual warfare, I dwell in divine peace, in Jesus' name.

9. I decree that the Lord establishes the works of my hands and causes all that I do to flourish and endure, in Jesus' name.

10. I decree that every area of my life previously marked by confusion, instability, or transience is now stabilized and fortified by the Word of God, in Jesus' name.

11. I decree that I am settled maritally, relationally, and emotionally; my life aligns with the divine plan for harmony and peace, in Jesus' name.

12. I decree that my roots go down deep, and my fruit rises upward, I am not scattered, but established as a pillar in God's kingdom, in Jesus' name.

13. I decree that every promise of settlement spoken over my life by prophecy and the Word of God begins to manifest speedily, in Jesus' name.

14. I decree that no man or demon shall displace me from my God-given territory, position, or

calling, in Jesus' name.

15. I decree that I am established in my identity in Christ and I walk in boldness, assurance, and confidence, in Jesus' name.

16. I decree that every legal ground used by the enemy to destabilize or unsettle me is revoked by the blood of Jesus, in Jesus' name.

17. I decree that I am settled in a land flowing with milk and honey, where my resources, relationships, and results align with divine abundance, in Jesus' name.

18. I decree that my foundations are healed and rebuilt upon Christ, the solid rock, my life shall no longer crumble or collapse, in Jesus' name.

19. I decree that divine stability, Favor, and peace will follow me and surround all that concerns me, in Jesus' name.

20. I decree that the Lord establishes me in righteousness, justice, and truth, and I shall not be moved, in Jesus' name.

CHAPTER 32

Delay, Stagnation, and Limitations

Delay is one of the enemy's most deceptive weapons. It doesn't stop you outright, it just slows you down, frustrates your purpose, and wears out your faith. Stagnation, likewise, keeps people stuck in the same place, repeating cycles and missing seasons of advancement. Limitations place invisible barriers that prevent breakthrough.

But God did not call you to a life of delay or limitation. He called you to move forward, to rise, to soar. Isaiah 60:1 says, "Arise, shine; for your light has come! And the glory of the Lord is risen upon you." Your destiny demands motion. Heaven is waiting for you to rise beyond the patterns that have confined you.

Jesus came to destroy every yoke. Through prophetic declarations, you can confront the spiritual forces behind delay, stagnation, and limitation. As you decree and declare, the power of God will break through every resistance, and you will gain divine speed and unstoppable progress.

You are not called to wander for 40 years in a journey that should take 11 days. You are not designed for dry places or closed gates. You were created to go from glory to glory. These declarations are for those who are tired of delay, weary of stagnation, and ready for forward motion in every area of life.

It's your time to move. It's your time to rise. It's your time to break free.

Key Scriptures:

- Isaiah 60:1 "Arise, shine; for your light has come!"
- Joel 2:25 "I will restore to you the years that the locust has eaten…"
- Deuteronomy 1:6 "You have dwelt long enough at this mountain."
- Job 22:28 "You shall also decree a thing, and it shall be established for you…"

Prophetic Declarations

1. I decree that every chain of delay holding back my progress is broken by the fire of God, and I advance swiftly into my destiny, in Jesus' name.

2. I decree that every spirit of stagnation operating in my life is arrested and permanently expelled by the power of the Holy Ghost, in Jesus' name.

3. I decree that I refuse to remain in the same position year after year, my story is changing, and I am moving forward, in Jesus' name.

4. I decree that divine acceleration is my portion; I overtake every delay and catch up with the divine timetable for my life, in Jesus' name.

5. I decree that the ancient gates of limitation in my foundation are shattered, and I walk in the freedom of Christ, in Jesus' name.

6. I decree that I am no longer tied down by fear, doubt, or generational cycles, I rise above every invisible barrier, in Jesus' name.

7. I decree that my destiny helpers are released to me without hindrance or interruption, in Jesus' name.

8. I decree that every embargo placed on my career, marriage, ministry, or business is lifted by the authority of the name of Jesus, in Jesus' name.

9. I decree that I am empowered to break records, set new standards, and fulfil my divine purpose without delay, in Jesus' name.

10. I decree that the spirit of "almost there but never arriving" is defeated and cast out of my life forever, in Jesus' name.

11. I decree that I will not be replaced or forgotten while waiting, I will possess my inheritance in due season, in Jesus' name.

12. I decree that every delay in my life is being turned into divine preparation for a greater manifestation, in Jesus' name.

13. I decree that closed doors are opening now, and I walk boldly into rooms where I was once denied access, in Jesus' name.

14. I decree that the yoke of limitation is broken off my life; I rise to fulfil my calling with speed and power, in Jesus' name.

15. I decree that I will not labour in vain; every

effort I make shall produce lasting results and divine reward, in Jesus' name.

16. I decree that no curse, spell, or evil word can keep me grounded, I soar by divine grace, in Jesus' name.

17. I decree that time is redeemed on my behalf, and every divine opportunity that passed me by is restored sevenfold, in Jesus' name.

18. I decree that I shall not be delayed in marriage, childbirth, promotion, ministry, or any good thing; divine alignment is my portion, in Jesus' name.

19. I decree that I shake off the dust of stagnation, and I step into the rivers of progress, abundance, and overflow, in Jesus' name.

20. I decree that this is my appointed time to rise, shine, and fulfil purpose without obstruction, in Jesus' name.

CHAPTER 33

Childlessness

Childlessness can be a deeply painful and private burden, often wrapped in silent tears and unspoken questions. For many, it represents not only a physical challenge but a spiritual battle that touches identity, faith, and hope. Yet, the Word of God is filled with promises for fruitfulness and the assurance that none shall be barren in His covenant.

From Sarah to Hannah to Elizabeth, the Bible shows us that God specializes in turning barrenness into fruitfulness. He hears the cries of the childless and responds with supernatural intervention. Psalm 113:9 says, "He makes the barren woman dwell in a house, as a joyful mother of children. Praise the Lord!" This is not just a poetic verse, it is a prophetic promise.

Every delay is not a denial, and every barren season has the potential for a miraculous testimony. The enemy uses childlessness to sow seeds of shame, comparison, and despair, but God's voice declares hope, healing, and fulfilment. As you decree and declare, you are not begging, you are enforcing your covenant rights.

Whether you are believing for biological children, spiritual children, or restoration after miscarriage or loss,

God is still the Giver of life. These declarations are crafted to break the chains of delay, open wombs, and silence every voice of accusation and hopelessness.

You are not forgotten. You are not forsaken. Your time of rejoicing is near. The God who remembered Rachel, who visited Hannah, and who honoured Elizabeth's faith, is the same yesterday, today, and forever.

Key Scriptures:

- Psalm 113:9 "He makes the barren woman a joyful mother of children."
- Genesis 1:28 "Be fruitful and multiply…"
- 1 Samuel 1:27 "For this child I prayed, and the Lord has granted me my petition…"
- Job 22:28 "You shall also decree a thing, and it shall be established for you…"
-

Prophetic Declarations

1. I decree that my womb, my body, and my life are fruitful and aligned with the divine mandate to be fruitful and multiply, in Jesus' name.

2. I decree that every label of barrenness placed on me is erased by the blood of Jesus, and I carry my evidence of fruitfulness, in Jesus' name.

3. I decree that every physical, medical, or spiritual cause of childlessness is uprooted by divine power of God, and I walk in supernatural conception, in Jesus' name.

4. I decree that no more delay, no more

disappointment, and no more sorrow, I enter into my season of joyful motherhood and fatherhood, in Jesus' name.

5. I decree that the same God who remembered Hannah, Sarah, and Elizabeth remembers me now and causes my womb to rejoice, in Jesus' name.

6. I decree that every curse of barrenness, spoken or inherited, is broken by the authority of Christ, and I carry my children to full term, in Jesus' name.

7. I decree that my home shall be filled with the sound of babies, and I shall nurture children who glorify the Lord, in Jesus' name.

8. I decree that I am not forgotten by God, His promise to make me fruitful and multiply me shall not fail, in Jesus' name.

9. I decree that healing and divine alignment take place in my reproductive system, and the hand of the Lord brings restoration, in Jesus' name.

10. I decree that I shall not be mocked or ashamed; my testimony shall silence every accuser and glorify God, in Jesus' name.

11. I decree that every fibroid, cyst, or blockage is dissolved by the fire of the Holy Ghost, and my body becomes a temple of fruitfulness, in Jesus' name.

12. I decree that the children I will bear are covenant children, anointed for signs and wonders, in Jesus' name.

13. I decree that every evil altar speaking against

my fruitfulness is silenced permanently, and my destiny as a joyful parent is established, in Jesus' name.

14. I decree that I reject fear, anxiety, and despair; I believe the report of the Lord concerning my fruitfulness, in Jesus' name.

15. I decree that divine Favor locates me, and the process of conception, pregnancy, and delivery shall be peaceful and victorious, in Jesus' name.

16. I decree that my partner and I are united in faith and love, and nothing shall hinder the blessing of children in our home, in Jesus' name.

17. I decree that angels are released to war against delay and to usher in my miracle babies, in Jesus' name.

18. I decree that my household shall experience supernatural fruitfulness beyond human limitation or diagnosis, in Jesus' name.

19. I decree that generational patterns of childlessness are broken with me, I begin a new lineage of fruitfulness and joy, in Jesus' name.

20. I decree that my season of sorrow is over; I carry my miracle babies and testify to the goodness of God, in Jesus' name.

CHAPTER 34

Long Life, Good Health, and Prosperity

God's desire for His children is not a life cut short, plagued by sickness or bound in poverty, but a full and fruitful existence filled with purpose, health, and divine supply. When we align with His Word, we tap into covenant promises that guarantee longevity, wellness, and abundance, not just for survival, but for thriving in every area of life.

Deuteronomy 30:19 says, "I have set before you life and death, blessing and cursing; therefore, choose life, that both you and your descendants may live." Choosing life includes embracing God's will for long days, divine vitality, and prosperity in spirit, soul, and body. It is your right through Christ.

Satan often attacks with premature death, mysterious illnesses, and financial frustration to steal peace and hinder destiny. But you are not helpless. As a child of God, you have been given authority to decree and declare life over your body, mind, and resources. Your words, spoken in faith, carry power to cancel demonic assignments and release divine Favor.

Psalm 91:16 assures us, "With long life I will satisfy him,

and show him My salvation." When you speak that Word in faith, you are activating divine insurance over your years and your health. Prosperity is not just financial gain; it is wholeness, nothing broken, nothing missing.

These prophetic declarations are your weapon and your shield. As you speak them, you are building a spiritual hedge around your life and future. Refuse the verdict of the enemy. Choose God's verdict, life, strength, and overflowing blessing.

Key Scriptures:

- Psalm 91:16 "With long life I will satisfy him..."
- 3 John 1:2 "I pray that you may prosper in all things and be in health..."
- Deuteronomy 30:19 "Choose life..."
- Job 22:28 "You shall also decree a thing, and it shall be established for you...

Prophetic Declarations

1. I decree that I shall live long and fulfil my divine purpose on earth; my life will not be cut short by sickness, accident, or premature death, in Jesus' name.

2. I decree that the Lord satisfies me with long life and shows me His salvation; I will not die but live to declare His works, in Jesus' name.

3. I decree that divine health is my portion, every cell, tissue, and organ in my body functions perfectly according to God's design, in Jesus' name.

4. I decree that I walk in supernatural strength, vitality, and energy, my youth is renewed like the eagle's, in Jesus' name.

5. I decree that the covenant of long life in Christ cancels every generational curse or evil prophecy of early death over me or my family, in Jesus' name.

6. I decree that sickness, disease, and infirmity will not thrive in my body; I am covered by the healing power of Jesus, in Jesus' name.

7. I decree that my household is preserved from tragedy, affliction, and calamity; we dwell in safety under the shadow of the Almighty, in Jesus' name.

8. I decree that every evil appointment with death is cancelled, and I walk in divine exemption from destruction, in Jesus' name.

9. I decree that prosperity flows into my life by divine Favor, I have more than enough to bless others and fulfil my calling, in Jesus' name.

10. I decree that I walk in financial abundance; lack, debt, and insufficiency are far from me, in Jesus' name.

11. I decree that the Lord blesses the work of my hands, and I prosper in all I do, in Jesus' name.

12. I decree that I operate in divine wisdom to manage, multiply, and maintain wealth for kingdom advancement, in Jesus' name.

13. I decree that I am fruitful in every season, spiritually, financially, mentally, and relationally, nothing withers in my life, in Jesus'

name.

14. I decree that I am a vessel of divine supply; I will lend to many and never borrow, in Jesus' name.

15. I decree that the windows of heaven are open over my life; divine ideas, opportunities, and Favor locate me without fail, in Jesus' name.

16. I decree that every curse of poverty, struggle, or financial failure is broken, and I step into generational blessings, in Jesus' name.

17. I decree that my health and wealth work together for the fulfilment of my God-ordained destiny, in Jesus' name.

18. I decree that unexpected blessings, promotions, and divine surprises locate me and overflow in my life, in Jesus' name.

19. I decree that I will leave an inheritance of wisdom, wealth, and righteousness for my children and their children, in Jesus' name.

20. I decree that my days on earth are prosperous, peaceful, powerful, and purposeful until I fulfil all that God has written concerning me, in Jesus' name.

CHAPTER 35

Favour

The Favor of God is a divine fragrance that sets you apart and causes doors to open where others are denied. It is the supernatural endorsement of heaven upon your life, attracting opportunities, kindness, promotion, and breakthroughs that cannot be explained by human effort. When God's Favor rests upon a person, protocols are suspended, rules are bypassed, and miracles happen with ease.

Psalm 5:12 declares, "For You, O Lord, will bless the righteous; with Favor, You will surround him as with a shield." God's Favor is not seasonal; it is meant to be a lifestyle. It goes before you to prepare the way, and it follows you to establish results. Favor will open doors that hard labour could never access. It brings divine connections, settlement, recognition, and lifting that defy logic.

Many people struggle because they rely on natural strategies alone. But Favor turns the ordinary into the extraordinary. When you decree and declare Favor over your life, you are aligning yourself with the will of God and summoning divine help to intervene in your affairs. Favor will cause your name to be mentioned in high places for good, release financial increase, and attract divine helpers.

Joseph found Favor in Potiphar's house (Genesis 39:4), Esther obtained Favor before the king (Esther 2:17), and Jesus increased in Favor with God and men (Luke 2:52). You too can walk in daily Favor. It is your inheritance in Christ.

Begin to decree and declare God's Favor over your life, your family, your business, your ministry, and your destiny. The tide is turning in your Favor.

Key Scriptures:

- Psalm 5:12 "With Favor, You will surround him as with a shield."
- Proverbs 3:4 "So you will find Favor and high esteem in the sight of God and man."
- Luke 2:52 "Jesus increased in wisdom and stature, and in Favor…"
- Job 22:28 "You shall also decree a thing, and it shall be established for you…"
-

Prophetic Declarations

1. I decree that I walk daily in divine favour, doors open for me effortlessly, and I am preferred above others, in Jesus' name.

2. I decree that the favour of God surrounds me like a shield and draws the right people, resources, and opportunities into my life, in Jesus' name.

3. I decree that wherever I go, favour will announce me, recommend me, and position me

for honour and elevation, in Jesus' name.

4. I decree that every form of rejection and disqualification is turned around by divine favour, and I am accepted and celebrated, in Jesus' name.

5. I decree that the favour of God distinguishes me in the marketplace, in ministry, and in every area of my life, in Jesus' name.

6. I decree that favour speaks louder than my weaknesses, background, or limitations, and I rise by grace, in Jesus' name.

7. I decree that kings and nobles favour me; I receive preferential treatment from people in high places, in Jesus' name.

8. I decree that favour breaks protocols on my behalf, and what takes other years shall be delivered to me in a moment, in Jesus' name.

9. I decree that I am highly favoured of the Lord; blessings locate me without struggle or manipulation, in Jesus' name.

10. I decree that favour opens doors of scholarships, contracts, positions, and connections that only God can orchestrate, in Jesus' name.

11. I decree that I am not just lucky, I am divinely positioned and strategically favoured for greatness, in Jesus' name.

12. I decree that favour terminates labour without result; I enter into the rest of God and enjoy supernatural increase, in Jesus' name.

13. I decree that favour follows my name, my applications, and my proposals, what others find

hard becomes easy for me, in Jesus' name.

14. I decree that my family, ministry, and business are saturated with the undeniable fragrance of God's favour, in Jesus' name.

15. I decree that favour defends me where I cannot speak for myself and fights battles, I do not even know exist, in Jesus' name.

16. I decree that my hands are blessed; wherever I lay them, favour flows and multiplies, in Jesus' name.

17. I decree that the delay I experienced is replaced with the speed of favour, I catch up and overtake, in Jesus' name.

18. I decree that the favour of God rewrites my story and positions me for divine remembrance and reward, in Jesus' name.

19. I decree that generational favour flows through me; my children and descendants shall walk in honour and dignity, in Jesus' name.

20. I decree that from today, I am a carrier of God's favour, unstoppable, unshakable, and overflowing in every area of my life, in Jesus' name.

CHAPTER 36

Evil Dreams

Dreams are a powerful channel of spiritual communication. God often speaks through dreams (Job 33:1416), but the enemy also uses dreams as a platform to sow fear, manipulation, affliction, and bondage. Evil dreams are not to be ignored, they can be demonic arrows, warnings, or indicators of spiritual attacks aimed at undermining your destiny.

The enemy knows that if he can infiltrate your dream life, he can plant seeds of destruction while you're unaware. Matthew 13:25 says, "But while men slept, his enemy came and sowed tares..." These tares can come in the form of nightmares, spiritual attacks, sexual dreams, eating in dreams, seeing dead relatives, or being pursued by animals or dark figures. All of these are red flags that something is wrong spiritually and must be addressed through prayer and prophetic decrees.

You must decree and declare your freedom from every evil manipulation through dreams. You have the power to cancel demonic dreams, reject satanic deposits, and reverse spiritual transactions carried out in your sleep. Through the blood of Jesus, you can purify your dream life and ensure only divine encounters are permitted.

Your sleep is meant to be peaceful and refreshing, not a battleground. According to Proverbs 3:24, "When you lie down, you will not be afraid; yes, you will lie down, and your sleep will be sweet." God's will is for your dreams to edify, instruct, and bless, not torment or imprison.

Take your authority. Declare war against evil dreams and recover everything stolen from you in the night. Your dream life is sanctified and secured by the power of God.

Key Scriptures:

- Matthew 13:25 "While men slept, his enemy came and sowed tares..."
- Job 33:14-16 "God speaks...in dreams, in visions of the night..."
- Proverbs 3:24 "Your sleep will be sweet."
- Job 22:28 "You shall also decree a thing, and it shall be established..."

Prophetic Declarations

1. I decree that every evil dream sent to plant fear, confusion, or destruction in my life is nullified by the blood of Jesus, in Jesus' name.

2. I decree that I am delivered from every satanic manipulation through dreams; no evil projection shall take root in my life, in Jesus' name.

3. I decree that I overcome and destroy every serpent, demon, or evil personality that appears in my dreams to attack my destiny, in Jesus' name.

4. I decree that no dream of backwardness, stagnation, or loss will manifest in my reality; I walk in divine progress, in Jesus' name.

5. I decree that every spirit husband, spirit wife, or marine agent appearing in my dreams is arrested by fire, and I am set free, in Jesus' name.

6. I decree that I receive divine fire and authority to cancel, reverse, and destroy every evil dream and its effects upon my life, in Jesus' name.

7. I decree that nightmares, sleep paralysis, and demonic visitations in the night are permanently terminated by the power of God, in Jesus' name.

8. I decree that no evil altar shall feed my spirit through dreams; I am covered and secured by the blood of Jesus, in Jesus' name.

9. I decree that every dream of death, accident, or disaster is cancelled, I shall live and not die, in Jesus' name.

10. I decree that my dream life is sanctified and controlled by the Holy Spirit; no evil entity shall manipulate my spiritual gates, in Jesus' name.

11. I decree that dreams sent to initiate me into covenants, pacts, or satanic altars are destroyed by the fire of God, in Jesus' name.

12. I decree that every recurring dream of shame, defeat, or captivity is broken, I walk in continuous freedom, in Jesus' name.

13. I decree that I receive divine insight and the gift of discerning dreams and visions; the enemy shall no longer deceive me, in Jesus' name.

14. I decree that every dream of eating, bathing, or receiving gifts from strange people is reversed and rendered powerless, in Jesus' name.

15. I decree that every ancestral spirit or family idol appearing in my dreams is consumed by Holy Ghost fire, in Jesus' name.

16. I decree that I shall no longer forget important divine dreams, my spiritual memory is restored and sharpened, in Jesus' name.

17. I decree that every power attacking me while I sleep is destroyed, and my nights become altars of encounter with God, in Jesus' name.

18. I decree that every evil observer or monitoring agent assigned to my dreams is blinded and silenced forever, in Jesus' name.

19. I decree that my dreams align with the Word and will of God; I receive revelation, instruction, and prophetic insight, in Jesus' name.

20. I decree that my sleep is peaceful, and no weapon formed against me through dreams shall prosper, in Jesus' name.

CHAPTER 37

Deliverance from Repeated
Failure and Setbacks

Repeated failure is not normal for a child of God. It is often a sign of spiritual interference, delay, or hidden altars working against progress. When you consistently face disappointment, whether in business, career, ministry, or relationships, it may be the result of a demonic cycle designed to frustrate your destiny and keep you from fulfilment.

God's will be not failure. According to Jeremiah 29:11, He has good plans for you, plans to prosper you and give you hope and a future. Yet many believers find themselves stuck in cycles of almost-success: getting close to breakthroughs but never fully receiving them, always starting but never finishing, being promised much but receiving little. This is not your inheritance in Christ.

Repeated failure and setbacks can be rooted in curses, foundational issues, or invisible barriers. But the good news is that you can break the cycle through the power of prayer and prophetic declarations. Decree and declare that every yoke of stagnation and failure is broken over your life. Speak divine acceleration into your journey. You are not meant to keep going around the same mountain.

Isaiah 43:19 says, "Behold, I will do a new thing; now it shall spring forth..." This is your season of newness, success, and forward movement. As you make these declarations, believe that your path is being straightened, your time is being redeemed, and your destiny is being restored.

You are not a failure. You are destined for greatness. Every delay is being overturned, and every setback is becoming a setup for your testimony.

Key Scriptures:

- Jeremiah 29:11 "For I know the thoughts that I think toward you...to give you a future and a hope."
- Isaiah 43:19 "Behold, I will do a new thing..."
- Proverbs 4:18 "The path of the righteous shines brighter..."
- Job 22:28 "You shall also decree a thing, and it shall be established..."

Prophetic Declarations

1. I decree that every cycle of repeated failure in my life is broken by the power in the blood of Jesus, I move forward with divine momentum, in Jesus' name.

2. I decree that every stronghold causing near-success syndrome and last-minute disappointment is destroyed by fire, in Jesus' name.

3. I decree that I am no longer a victim of rising

and falling; I walk in consistent progress and victory, in Jesus' name.

4. I decree that the hand of the Lord lifts me above every force of delay, stagnation, and backwardness, in Jesus' name.

5. I decree that I break out of every pattern of failure established by ancestral covenants and evil foundations, in Jesus' name.

6. I decree that divine acceleration overtakes every past delay, I recover wasted years and lost opportunities, in Jesus' name.

7. I decree that every demonic trap set to sabotage my efforts and bring shame is exposed and destroyed, in Jesus' name.

8. I decree that I am delivered from the curse of "almost there but never arriving" I enter fully into my breakthroughs, in Jesus' name.

9. I decree that the spirit of confusion and error is removed from my path; I receive clarity, direction, and success, in Jesus' name.

10. I decree that I no longer labour in vain or plant for another to reap, my work produces fruit, and I enjoy the harvest, in Jesus' name.

11. I decree that the Lord crowns my efforts with divine favour and success; rejection and denial are replaced with acceptance and promotion, in Jesus' name.

12. I decree that I excel in every area where I once failed; I am anointed to rise beyond former limits, in Jesus' name.

13. I decree that the reproach of my past failures

is rolled away; I enter into a season of new beginnings, in Jesus' name.

14. I decree that no evil pattern from my family line will repeat itself in my life; I am a new creation in Christ, in Jesus' name.

15. I decree that every demonic delay assigned to frustrate my destiny is arrested and cast out of my life, in Jesus' name.

16. I decree that the spirit of excellence rests upon me; I succeed where others fall, and I stand firm in purpose, in Jesus' name.

17. I decree that the blood of Jesus wipes away every spiritual handwriting of limitation and failure working against me, in Jesus' name.

18. I decree that I receive supernatural strength, wisdom, and strategy to advance without hindrance, in Jesus' name.

19. I decree that the chains of failure and disappointment are broken; I walk boldly into God's open doors, in Jesus' name.

20. I decree that my life is moving from failure to favour, from breakdown to breakthrough, from defeat to dominion, in Jesus' name.

CHAPTER 38

Deliverance from Depression and Oppression

Depression and oppression are silent tormentors that aim to cripple the soul, drain hope, and silence faith. They often appear as dark clouds of heaviness, fear, worthlessness, or despair. While the world may treat depression as only a mental health condition, the Bible reveals that it can also be a spiritual battle, one that the enemy uses to wear down and imprison God's people.

But take heart: God has not left you helpless. Isaiah 61:3 says He gives "the garment of praise for the spirit of heaviness." The Word of God reveals a divine exchange: your sorrow for His joy, your mourning for His comfort, your weakness for His strength.

Depression thrives in silence and isolation, but breakthrough comes when you begin to decree and declare your freedom in Christ. The Holy Spirit is the Comforter, and His presence brings peace that surpasses understanding. No matter how deep the pit may feel, there is a hand of mercy ready to lift you out.

Spiritual oppression can come through fear, curses, generational bondage, or traumatic events. But Jesus came to set the captives free. He said in Luke 4:18, "He has sent Me to heal the broken-hearted, to proclaim liberty to the captives..." You are not forgotten, and you are not powerless.

Use the declarations in this chapter with boldness. Speak life over your mind, soul, and emotions. God's joy is your strength. The darkness cannot prevail when the Light of Christ shines through.

Key Scriptures:

- Isaiah 61:3 "To give them... the garment of praise for the spirit of heaviness..."
- Luke 4:18 "To set at liberty those who are oppressed..."
- Nehemiah 8:10 "The joy of the Lord is your strength."
- Job 22:28 "You shall also decree a thing, and it shall be established..."

Prophetic Declarations

1. I decree that every weight of depression, heaviness, and darkness over my mind is lifted and destroyed by the power of the Holy Spirit, in Jesus' name.

2. I decree that the joy of the Lord is my strength, I arise from every pit of despair into the light of hope and peace, in Jesus' name.

3. I decree that every oppressive thought and lying voice whispering defeat, failure, and worthlessness is silenced by the blood of Jesus, in Jesus' name.

4. I decree that I receive the garment of praise instead of the spirit of heaviness; I dance in victory over sorrow, in Jesus' name.

5. I decree that I am not hopeless, I am loved, chosen, and upheld by God's unfailing hand, in Jesus' name.

6. I decree that my mind is healed, my emotions are restored, and I walk in the soundness and wholeness of Christ, in Jesus' name.

7. I decree that no force of darkness can cage my soul; I break free from emotional captivity and mental torment, in Jesus' name.

8. I decree that I am filled with the peace of God that surpasses all understanding, my heart and mind are guarded in Christ Jesus, in Jesus' name.

9. I decree that the blood of Jesus cleanses me from every trauma, sorrow, and emotional wound, I am made whole, in Jesus' name.

10. I decree that every spirit of suicide, hopelessness, and self-hate loses its hold over me now, I choose life, in Jesus' name.

11. I decree that I receive divine clarity and renewal; my mind is not a battlefield for the enemy but a sanctuary for the Spirit of God, in Jesus' name.

12. I decree that I walk in the light of truth and cast off every lie of the enemy that seeks to drag me into darkness, in Jesus' name.

13. I decree that my emotions come under the lordship of Jesus Christ, I feel what He feels and know the peace He gives, in Jesus' name.

14. I decree that every generational oppression or

inherited emotional bondage is broken by the anointing of the Holy Ghost, in Jesus' name.

15. I decree that laughter fills my mouth and singing fills my soul, the days of mourning and sorrow are over, in Jesus' name.

16. I decree that the Spirit of life in Christ Jesus has set me free from every death sentence over my mental and emotional health, in Jesus' name.

17. I decree that my nights are filled with peaceful sleep and not torment, my dreams are pure, restful, and divinely inspired, in Jesus' name.

18. I decree that I am not isolated or abandoned, I am deeply connected to God and surrounded by His love, in Jesus' name.

19. I decree that every chain of mental oppression, anxiety, and inner turmoil is shattered; I receive the oil of gladness, in Jesus' name.

20. I decree that I am completely free from depression and oppression, I rise and shine because my light has come, in Jesus' name.

CHAPTER 39

Blessings

God delights in blessing His children. From the beginning of creation, His heart has been to bless, multiply, and empower His people. The word blessing signifies divine Favor, increase, abundance, peace, and fruitfulness in every area of life. When you walk in covenant with God, blessings are not just possible, they are your inheritance.

Deuteronomy 28:2 declares, "And all these blessings shall come upon you and overtake you, because you obey the voice of the Lord your God." These blessings are not passive. They actively pursue the believer who walks by faith and obedience. God's blessings encompass your health, relationships, finances, destiny, and peace of mind.

But blessings are not automatic. They must be claimed, declared, and walked in. Life and death are in the power of the tongue (Proverbs 18:21), so when you decree God's Word over your life, you release angelic activity and heavenly alignment. You speak your atmosphere into agreement with divine promises.

These declarations will help you break free from every curse and limitation and usher you into the realm of divine blessings. You are not under the curse. You are blessed beyond measure. You are blessed in the city, in the field, in your going out and coming in. You are blessed spiritually, physically, emotionally, and financially.

Decree and declare the blessings of God over your life with boldness. As you do, expect the Favor of God to locate you and elevate you.

Key Scriptures:

- Deuteronomy 28:2 "All these blessings shall come upon you and overtake you..."
- Proverbs 10:22 "The blessing of the Lord makes one rich, and He adds no sorrow with it."
- Ephesians 1:3 "Blessed... with every spiritual blessing in the heavenly places..."
- Job 22:28 "You shall also decree a thing, and it shall be established..."

Prophetic Declarations

1. I decree that I am blessed beyond measure, the hand of the Lord rests upon me, and His favour surrounds me like a shield, in Jesus' name.

2. I decree that the blessing of the Lord makes me rich and adds no sorrow; lack and insufficiency are far from me, in Jesus' name.

3. I decree that I walk in the blessing of Abraham, Isaac, and Jacob; my covenant with God positions me for generational prosperity, in Jesus' name.

4. I decree that I am blessed in the city and blessed in the field; my going out and coming in are

divinely favoured, in Jesus' name.

5. I decree that the blessings of open doors, divine opportunities, and supernatural favour locate me daily, in Jesus' name.

6. I decree that the blessing of wisdom, understanding, and sound judgment rests on me; I do not walk in error, in Jesus' name.

7. I decree that my hands are blessed; everything I touch prospers, multiplies, and flourishes by God's grace, in Jesus' name.

8. I decree that my family is blessed, peace, love, and unity reign in my home, in Jesus' name.

9. I decree that I am blessed with good health; sickness and affliction have no place in my body, in Jesus' name.

10. I decree that my children are blessed; they are mighty in the land and fulfil their divine assignments, in Jesus' name.

11. I decree that I am blessed with divine protection; no weapon formed against me shall prosper, in Jesus' name.

12. I decree that the blessings of divine ideas, creativity, and innovation are released upon me; I excel in all I do, in Jesus' name.

13. I decree that I am blessed with supernatural breakthroughs; barriers and limitations are shattered before me, in Jesus' name.

14. I decree that the blessing of divine restoration is my portion; all I have lost is returned to me sevenfold, in Jesus' name.

15. I decree that I am a carrier of God's blessing,

wherever I go, lives are impacted and changed, in Jesus' name.

16. I decree that I am blessed with financial favour; doors of provision and abundance open for me without struggle, in Jesus' name.

17. I decree that I am blessed with divine peace, my mind is calm, my heart is steady, and my soul is anchored in Christ, in Jesus' name.

18. I decree that my past mistakes do not cancel my blessings; grace speaks for me and lifts me into new realms, in Jesus' name.

19. I decree that my cup overflows with blessings, I have more than enough to bless others and advance the Kingdom, in Jesus' name.

20. I decree that I walk in perpetual blessing; every day brings new testimonies and undeniable favour, in Jesus' name.

CHAPTER 40

Unemployment

Unemployment can be a deeply discouraging and frustrating experience. It can challenge your confidence, strain your finances, and test your faith. But as a child of God, you are not forsaken or forgotten. God sees your need and has a plan for your provision. His Word promises that He will supply all your needs according to His riches in glory (Philippians 4:19).

In times of joblessness, the enemy may try to sow lies, whispers of failure, rejection, or worthlessness. But you must stand firm and decree and declare your identity and destiny in Christ. You are not unemployed; you are being prepared. You are not overlooked; you are being strategically positioned.

God is a master at turning what looks like a setback into a setup for greater promotion. David was tending sheep when he was called to be king. Joseph went from the prison to the palace. Your current condition is not your conclusion. As you speak life into your situation, doors will open, Favor will be released, and divine connections will be orchestrated.

These declarations will release supernatural Favor, divine recommendations, and open doors for employment, contracts, and career advancement. You are not begging for scraps; you are royalty accessing your inheritance.

Begin to decree and declare employment breakthroughs over your life. You will walk into rooms you didn't apply for, receive offers you didn't expect, and step into roles that exceed your qualifications, in Jesus' name.

Key Scriptures:

- Philippians 4:19 "My God shall supply all your need…"
- Psalm 75:67 "Promotion comes neither from the east nor from the west… but God is the judge…"
- Isaiah 45:23 "I will go before you… I will give you the treasures of darkness…"
- Job 22:28 "You shall also decree a thing, and it shall be established…"
-

Prophetic Declarations

1. I decree that every door of gainful employment shut against me is now opened by divine power of Holy Spirit, in Jesus' name.
2. I decree that I am not jobless, I am positioned for divine placement and supernatural opportunities, in Jesus' name.
3. I decree that my CV, applications, and qualifications receive divine attention and favour where it matters most, in Jesus' name.
4. I decree that I am connected to the right people, at the right time, for the right opportunities that

align with my purpose, in Jesus' name.

5. I decree that the spirit of rejection and delay is broken over my job search; acceptance and speed locate me, in Jesus' name.

6. I decree that employers are compelled by the hand of God to remember me and call me forth, in Jesus' name.

7. I decree that I shall not beg to survive, I walk in the dignity of labour and the abundance of divine supply, in Jesus' name.

8. I decree that I receive divine wisdom, ideas, and inspiration to create wealth and not depend solely on man, in Jesus' name.

9. I decree that I am favoured above others for roles I am qualified and unqualified for, God qualifies me where man disqualifies me, in Jesus' name.

10. I decree that any spiritual embargo on my career or work life is shattered by fire, in Jesus' name.

11. I decree that I break free from cycles of disappointment, silence, and missed opportunities in the job market, in Jesus' name.

12. I decree that my season of divine employment and fruitful labour is now; I step into it with boldness, in Jesus' name.

13. I decree that my hands will not be idle, God blesses the work of my hands and establishes me, in Jesus' name.

14. I decree that I receive calls, emails, and messages of job offers and open doors this season, in Jesus' name.

15. I decree that I am empowered to be productive,

useful, and impactful in my generation, in Jesus' name.

16. I decree that I break out from the label of "unemployed" into a new identity of "employed by favour," in Jesus' name.

17. I decree that every interview I attend turns into a testimony of divine selection, in Jesus' name.

18. I decree that the atmosphere over my career is shifted and saturated with angelic help and divine orchestration, in Jesus' name.

19. I decree that my job is not delayed, it is released, manifesting now by the command of heaven, in Jesus' name.

20. I decree that my destiny helpers arise and locate me with opportunities that will establish my financial stability, in Jesus' name.

CHAPTER 41

Youths

The youth are not just the leaders of tomorrow; they are God's instruments for today. The enemy knows the power and potential of young people, which is why he targets them with confusion, identity crises, rebellion, addiction, sexual immorality, and purposelessness. But the Word of God declares that young men and women will see visions and prophesy (Joel 2:28), and that they are strong and overcome the wicked one (1 John 2:14).

God is raising a new generation of firebrands, reformers, and revivalists who will carry His power and proclaim His truth. Decree and declare that the youth in your life, your children, students, mentees, or even your younger self, will not be swallowed by this world but will shine as lights in the darkness.

Now more than ever, our declarations matter. We must speak life over our youth, declaring that they will fulfil destiny, love righteousness, and walk in wisdom. We declare their minds are sound, their hearts are pure, and their feet are ordered by the Lord. They will not be confused or lost but aligned with God's purpose from an early age.

These prophetic declarations are weapons of warfare to cancel rebellion, restore identity, unlock potential, and release divine encounters upon the youth. As you decree and declare these truths, expect a revival to break out in homes, schools, churches, and communities.

Don't give up on the youth, pray, prophesy, and declare God's Word over them. They shall live and not die; they shall serve the Lord with gladness.

Key Scriptures:

- Joel 2:28 "Your sons and your daughters shall prophesy..."
- 1 John 2:14 "You are strong, and the word of God abides in you..."
- Proverbs 22:6 "Train up a child in the way he should go..."
- Job 22:28 "You shall also decree a thing, and it shall be established..."

Prophetic Declarations

1. I decree that the youths of this generation are set apart for God's purpose, they will not be wasted by the enemy, in Jesus' name.

2. I decree that I am a youth on fire for God, rooted in righteousness, and filled with the Holy Spirit, in Jesus' name.

3. I decree that every assignment of darkness to derail, distract, or destroy the destinies of young people is frustrated and cancelled, in Jesus' name.

4. I decree that I carry divine wisdom, discipline, and discernment; I do not follow the crowd, I follow Christ, in Jesus' name.

5. I decree that I rise as a voice of truth, leadership, and purpose among my generation, in Jesus' name.

6. I decree that the chains of addiction, sexual immorality, peer pressure, and identity confusion are broken over every youth, in Jesus' name.

7. I decree that I am not a statistic of failure or destruction, I am a living testimony of grace and glory, in Jesus' name.

8. I decree that every youth under oppression, depression, or suicidal thoughts is delivered and healed by the power of the Holy Ghost, in Jesus' name.

9. I decree that God is raising youth revivalists, evangelists, prophets, and kingdom influencers who will shake this generation for Christ, in Jesus' name.

10. I decree that I pursue holiness, not popularity, obedience, not rebellion, and I walk with God all my days, in Jesus' name.

11. I decree that I reject every label, lie, and limitation placed on me by society or culture, I wear God's identity, in Jesus' name.

12. I decree that no youth in my family or community shall be lost to crime, gangs, occultism, or premature death, in Jesus' name.

13. I decree that God is pouring out His Spirit upon us as young men and women, we prophesy, dream dreams, and do mighty exploits, in Jesus' name.

14. I decree that I will not waste my youth chasing vanity, I invest it in building a strong spiritual and purposeful foundation, in Jesus' name.

15. I decree that every gift, talent, and calling in me comes alive and finds full expression under the guidance of the Holy Spirit, in Jesus' name.

16. I decree that I am divinely exempted from societal corruption, trends of perversion, and the seductions of this age, in Jesus' name.

17. I decree that I walk in financial wisdom and integrity, I shall not be enslaved by poverty or wealth, but empowered by stewardship, in Jesus' name.

18. I decree that I rise above every limitation set by my background, education, or environment, I walk in kingdom elevation, in Jesus' name.

19. I decree that I am a role model of righteousness, faith, and courage; others see Christ in me and follow, in Jesus' name.

20. I decree that the future belongs to God's youth, and I take my place as a light in the midst of darkness, in Jesus' name.

CHAPTER 42

Stubborn Problems

Some battles in life are not easily won. They linger for months, years, or even generations. These are what we call stubborn problems, situations that defy human wisdom, resist prayer, and seem immovable despite fasting and intercession. They manifest as chronic sicknesses, financial hardship, generational curses, delayed marriages, long-term barrenness, or cycles of failure. But no matter how long a problem has stood, the power of God is greater and can bring it down in a moment.

When Pharaoh refused to let Israel go, God responded with divine judgment. It took persistent declarations, power confrontations, and unwavering faith to bring down that stubborn system of oppression. Likewise, through prophetic decrees, we enforce our authority in Christ over every stubborn situation in our lives.

It is time to decree and declare that every Pharaoh must fall, every Red Sea must part, and every Jericho wall must collapse. Your voice carries the authority of heaven when aligned with the Word of God. These declarations are spiritual bulldozers, levelling mountains, uprooting demonic altars, and making crooked paths straight.

Don't normalize or settle with what God never ordained for you. Rise up and speak with boldness! God has given you the power to decree a thing, and it shall be established. Every stubborn problem bows to the name of Jesus.

Key Scriptures:

- Jeremiah 32:27 "Behold, I am the Lord, the God of all flesh. Is there anything too hard for Me?"
- Matthew 17:20 "If you have faith as a mustard seed... nothing will be impossible for you."
- Exodus 14:13-14 "The Lord will fight for you, and you shall hold your peace."
- Job 22:28 "You shall also decree a thing, and it shall be established..."
-

Prophetic Declarations

1. I decree that every stubborn problem resisting prayer, fasting, and prophetic instruction in my life bows to the power of the Almighty, in Jesus' name.

2. I decree that ancient battles and recurring afflictions are broken today by the blood of Jesus, in Jesus' name.

3. I decree that every stronghold of delay, disease, or despair in my life is uprooted and destroyed forever, in Jesus' name.

4. I decree that what has remained stagnant for years suddenly shifts by divine intervention and

angelic force, in Jesus' name.

5. I decree that the God who parted the Red Sea and raised the dead is solving every stubborn issue in my life right now, in Jesus' name.

6. I decree that spiritual mountains standing in the way of my joy, peace, and progress are removed by fire, in Jesus' name.

7. I decree that stubborn foundational powers fuelling my battles are consumed by the fire of God, in Jesus' name.

8. I decree that I escape every cycle of failure, frustration, and disappointment that has persisted for years, in Jesus' name.

9. I decree that stubborn patterns in my family line end with me, I walk in victory and freedom, in Jesus' name.

10. I decree that demonic verdicts and satanic decrees over my life are reversed by the voice of the blood, in Jesus' name.

11. I decree that my destiny is too fiery to be caged by any stubborn bondage or spiritual prison, in Jesus' name.

12. I decree that I receive divine strategy and supernatural wisdom to deal with every problem mocking my prayers, in Jesus' name.

13. I decree that I shall not give up, I receive renewed strength to wrestle until I prevail like Jacob, in Jesus' name.

14. I decree that no stubborn enemy shall triumph over me; I walk in total dominion, in Jesus' name.

15. I decree that battles that defeated others in my lineage will not defeat my, I am more than a conqueror, in Jesus' name.

16. I decree that what was impossible for me before becomes possible now by the power of the Most High, in Jesus' name.

17. I decree that stubborn afflictions in my body or mind disappear completely under the authority of Jesus' name, in Jesus' name.

18. I decree that the spirit behind stubborn resistance is arrested, judged, and cast out of my life forever, in Jesus' name.

19. I decree that long-standing shame, reproach, and disgrace are replaced with glory, celebration, and divine lifting, in Jesus' name.

20. I decree that today marks the end of stubborn limitations in my life, I walk in total freedom and victory, in Jesus' name.

CHAPTER 43

Evil Charms, Sacrifices, and Incantations

In the realm of the spirit, wicked people use physical items and spoken words to manipulate destinies, afflict lives, and hinder God's blessings. Evil charms, demonic sacrifices, and satanic incantations are tools used by the enemy to summon spirits, enforce curses, and cause mysterious attacks. These are not myths, they are real spiritual weapons used by dark agents to tie destinies down, invoke affliction, or exchange glory.

However, as children of God, we are not helpless. We are seated with Christ in heavenly places, far above all principalities and powers (Ephesians 1:2021). No charm, sacrifice, or incantation can override the blood of Jesus or nullify the authority we carry in His name. Every incantation spoken against you must fall to the ground powerless. Every charm buried, burnt, or placed in secret to bind you shall be rendered useless.

It's time to decree and declare your victory over all satanic operations. As you release prophetic declarations, angelic forces are dispatched to destroy evil altars, reverse demonic verdicts, and silence every voice speaking against you. No demonic enchantment or divination will prosper when the fire of God answers on your behalf.

Rise in your God-given authority and scatter the plans of the wicked. Every evil hand raised against your life shall wither, and every mouth speaking evil shall be silenced by divine judgment.

Key Scriptures:

- Numbers 23:23 "For there is no enchantment against Jacob, neither is there any divination against Israel."
- Isaiah 54:17 "No weapon formed against you shall prosper, and every tongue... you shall condemn."
- Job 22:28 "You shall also decree a thing, and it shall be established..."
- Psalm 68:1 "Let God arise, let His enemies be scattered..."

Prophetic Declarations

1. I decree that every evil charm fashioned against my life, destiny, or family is rendered powerless and destroyed by the fire of the Holy Ghost, in Jesus' name.

2. I decree that every sacrifice made on any altar to hinder or afflict me is reversed and consumed by the blood of Jesus, in Jesus' name.

3. I decree that I am covered by the covenant of the blood of Jesus, and no evil incantation or spell shall work against me, in Jesus' name.

4. I decree that I escape every trap set by witches, sorcerers, or enchanters seeking to manipulate or harm me, in Jesus' name.

5. I decree that every demonic altar crying against my name or destiny is silenced and scattered without recovery, in Jesus' name.

6. I decree that no charm buried, spoken, or activated against me shall prosper, I walk in divine immunity, in Jesus' name.

7. I decree that every blood sacrifice and invocation made to monitor, delay, or frustrate me backfires now, in Jesus' name.

8. I decree that every item representing me in evil places catches fire and is turned to ashes, in Jesus' name.

9. I decree that my life is not subject to enchantment or divination, I am covered by the blood and shielded by God's power, in Jesus' name.

10. I decree that I am not a victim of ancestral rituals or generational incantations; I am redeemed and free, in Jesus' name.

11. I decree that any spoken curse or ritual declaration against my marriage, health, finances, or children is nullified by the power in the name of Jesus, in Jesus' name.

12. I decree that no evil priest, herbalist, or occult agent has the final say over my destiny, God alone determines my path, in Jesus' name.

13. I decree that I walk out of every evil cage where I've been spiritually locked by charms or

sacrifices, in Jesus' name.

14. I decree that every monitoring power assigned through rituals or dark utterances to track me is struck blind and confused, in Jesus' name.

15. I decree that the fire of God visits every evil junction where my name has been submitted for destruction, in Jesus' name.

16. I decree that my dreams, progress, and prayers shall no longer be hindered by demonic tokens or sacrifices, in Jesus' name.

17. I decree that every evil pot, calabash, or charm being used to manipulate my destiny breaks and scatters by divine thunder, in Jesus' name.

18. I decree that no enchantment or divination shall hold me bound again, I am loosed permanently, in Jesus' name.

19. I decree that the power of Jesus Christ speaks louder than any dark incantation made against me or my family, in Jesus' name.

20. I decree that my life, home, business, and ministry are surrounded by divine fire and cannot be penetrated by evil charms or sacrifices, in Jesus' name.

CHAPTER 44

Evil Herbalists

Throughout history and even today, many people unknowingly or ignorantly consult herbalists or traditional spiritualists in search of healing, help, or protection. While some herbalists deal strictly with natural medicine, evil herbalists mix rituals, incantations, and demonic powers to manipulate situations and bind souls. These individuals serve as channels of demonic influence, often invoking spirits, crafting potions, and preparing charms that place people under bondage instead of bringing true healing or deliverance.

The enemy uses such vessels to entangle people in spiritual webs, causing cycles of misfortune, illness, barrenness, financial hardship, and marital turmoil. Many destinies have been tied down on demonic altars through consultations with evil herbalists. But no power, no shrine, no demonic altar can stand before the blood of Jesus Christ.

As a child of God, you are empowered to decree and declare freedom from every covenant, enchantment, or curse released through these dark agents. The fire of God will locate and consume every evil work done against you by any herbalist or spiritualist. Every pot, calabash, mirror, or shrine used to monitor or manipulate your life shall catch fire and be destroyed.

Through prophetic declarations, you can command divine judgment upon evil altars and recover everything stolen or exchanged in the spirit. You are covered by the blood of Jesus and shielded by divine fire.

Key Scriptures:

- Micah 5:12 "I will cut off witchcrafts out of thine hand; and thou shalt have no more soothsayers."
- Isaiah 44:25 "He frustrates the signs of the babblers, and drives diviners mad..."
- Job 22:28 "You shall also decree a thing, and it shall be established for you..."
- Galatians 5:1 "Stand fast therefore in the liberty wherewith Christ hath made us free..."
-

Prophetic Declarations

1. I decree that every evil herbalist consulting demonic spirits against me falls into their own trap and their powers turn to confusion, in Jesus' name.

2. I decree that the blood of Jesus renders every concoction, potion, or mixture from evil herbalists powerless over my life, in Jesus' name.

3. I decree that my name, photo, or any item connected to me shall not be used successfully in any herbalist shrine or altar, in Jesus' name.

4. I decree that every evil agenda orchestrated by

herbalists, diviners, or fetish priests to destroy my life is reversed by the fire of God, in Jesus' name.

5. I decree that I am not a candidate for diabolical consultation, I am covered by the fire of the Holy Ghost, in Jesus' name.

6. I decree that every evil spoken word, incantation, or ritual released by a herbalist against my destiny is cancelled by the superior blood of Jesus, in Jesus' name.

7. I decree that every herbalist manipulating time, seasons, and opportunities in my life is exposed and judged by God, in Jesus' name.

8. I decree that my household is too hot for satanic interference; no demonic herbalist can succeed against us, in Jesus' name.

9. I decree that I shall not be a victim of spiritual transactions made on evil altars by herbalists, in Jesus' name.

10. I decree that all evil assignments given to herbalists to stop my progress are terminated by divine authority, in Jesus' name.

11. I decree that my glory and virtue are hidden in Christ and cannot be accessed or tampered with by any evil power, in Jesus' name.

12. I decree that the fire of the Lord pursues and consumes every evil herbalist working behind the scenes to delay my breakthrough, in Jesus' name.

13. I decree that the territory I dwell in is sanctified and protected; no herbalist can operate against

me within or outside, in Jesus' name.

14. I decree that every herbalist operating in my family line loses their influence and spiritual grip over our destinies, in Jesus' name.

15. I decree that my health shall not be afflicted by any evil substance, oil, or ritual released by herbal hands, in Jesus' name.

16. I decree that wherever my name has been taken by herbalists, the angels of the Lord are sent now to retrieve and deliver me, in Jesus' name.

17. I decree that the evil herbalist operating in secret places with my information is exposed and disgraced publicly, in Jesus' name.

18. I decree that no herbalist shall have peace or progress while they continue to work wickedness against the children of God, in Jesus' name.

19. I decree that every source of power and backup for evil herbalists is dried up and permanently destroyed, in Jesus' name.

20. I decree that the Lord is my deliverer and defender, no herbalist can match the power of Jehovah over my life, in Jesus' name.

CHAPTER 45

Addictions

Addictions are powerful chains that bind the soul, body, and spirit. Whether it's addiction to substances, harmful behaviours, sexual immorality, pornography, social media, gambling, or food, these strongholds often grow silently but deeply. Many people, including believers, suffer under the grip of addiction, feeling helpless, ashamed, and disconnected from God's purpose for their lives.

Addiction is not just a habit; it's a spiritual bondage that requires spiritual intervention. Behind every destructive addiction is a demonic force that seeks to enslave, distract, and ultimately destroy. But thank God for the power in the name of Jesus! Deliverance is possible, healing is available, and restoration is assured for those who cry out to God in faith.

You must decree and declare your freedom, renouncing every demonic hold over your will, mind, and body. The blood of Jesus breaks every yoke, and the anointing destroys every chain. God is not ashamed of you; He longs to heal and restore you. Every declaration you speak in faith will shatter the enemy's grip and reposition you for a life of holiness and purpose.

Declare war on addiction. Don't stay silent. Don't accept the lie that you can't be free. You are not powerless, you are a child of the Most High God, and through Christ, you have dominion. Freedom is your covenant right.

Key Scriptures:

- Romans 6:14 "For sin shall not have dominion over you…"
- Isaiah 10:27 "The yoke shall be destroyed because of the anointing."
- John 8:36 "Therefore if the Son makes you free, you shall be free indeed."
- Job 22:28 "You shall also decree a thing, and it shall be established for you…"

Prophetic Declarations

1. I decree that every addiction, whether physical, emotional, or spiritual, loses its grip over my life right now by the power of the Holy Spirit, in Jesus' name.
2. I decree that I am no longer a slave to habits that damage my body, mind, or destiny, I walk in total freedom, in Jesus' name.
3. I decree that the desire for anything unholy or harmful is uprooted from my life and replaced with the hunger for righteousness, in Jesus' name.
4. I decree that cycles of secret struggles, shame, and defeat are broken forever by the anointing that destroys yokes, in Jesus' name.

5. I decree that the Spirit of God empowers me to say no to every destructive craving and temptation, in Jesus' name.

6. I decree that I am not defined by my past or weaknesses, I rise above every form of bondage, in Jesus' name.

7. I decree that every spirit behind addiction, be it lust, substance, media, food, gambling, or secrecy, is cast out of my life, in Jesus' name.

8. I decree that I walk daily in discipline, self-control, and the fear of the Lord, in Jesus' name.

9. I decree that the blood of Jesus cleanses my body, soul, and mind from every residue of addiction, in Jesus' name.

10. I decree that I shall not be held back from fulfilling destiny because of hidden bondage, my freedom is secured, in Jesus' name.

11. I decree that every stronghold in my mind fuelling addictive patterns is demolished by truth and revelation, in Jesus' name.

12. I decree that my body is the temple of the Holy Spirit and shall no longer be desecrated by unholy habits, in Jesus' name.

13. I decree that supernatural help, accountability, and healing are released into my life as I pursue lasting deliverance, in Jesus' name.

14. I decree that I no longer suppress pain or trauma with substances or sin, I am healed at the root, in Jesus' name.

15. I decree that every portal through which the enemy fuels addiction in my life is sealed

permanently by the blood of Jesus, in Jesus' name.

16. I decree that the hold of addiction over my family line is broken with me, I set a new generational standard, in Jesus' name.

17. I decree that I am filled with joy, peace, and purpose, no substitute or counterfeit shall lure me again, in Jesus' name.

18. I decree that I walk in newness of life, and the chains of addiction will not follow me into my next season, in Jesus' name.

19. I decree that I shall testify of my total freedom and use my story to set others free, in Jesus' name.

20. I decree that I am free, completely delivered, and wholly restored by the mercy and power of God, in Jesus' name.

CHAPTER 46

Mental Illnesses

Mental illness is a real and growing concern in our world, one that affects people of all ages, races, and backgrounds. Depression, anxiety, bipolar disorder, schizophrenia, post-traumatic stress disorder (PTSD), suicidal thoughts, and emotional instability are just some of the battles many quietly face. But as a child of God, you must know that mental illness is not your identity. You are not forgotten, forsaken, or permanently broken. God is your Healer, body, soul, and mind.

Scripture clearly shows that peace of mind is part of your inheritance in Christ. Jesus came to set the captives free, to heal the broken-hearted, and to give beauty for ashes. The enemy often targets the mind because it is the battlefield of the soul. Through trauma, generational curses, abuse, rejection, and spiritual attacks, the devil tries to cloud your thoughts, steal your joy, and lead you into despair.

But the Word of God renews the mind. The blood of Jesus silences torment. The Holy Spirit brings comfort and clarity. God has not given you a spirit of fear, confusion, or heaviness, but of power, love, and a sound mind.

It's time to decree and declare your mental wholeness.

Every lying thought, every tormenting spirit, every chemical imbalance, and every emotional wound must bow to the authority of Jesus Christ. Healing is possible. Peace is your portion.

As you boldly speak these prophetic declarations, expect clarity, deliverance, and divine restoration in your mental and emotional life.

Key Scriptures:

- 2 Timothy 1:7 "For God has not given us a spirit of fear, but of power and of love and of a sound mind."
- Isaiah 26:3 "You will keep him in perfect peace, whose mind is stayed on You."
- Job 22:28 "You shall also decree a thing, and it shall be established for you..."
-

Prophetic Declarations

1. I decree that every attack on my mind, whether through trauma, anxiety, depression, or confusion, is broken by the power of God, in Jesus' name.

2. I decree that I have the mind of Christ, I think clearly, soundly, and wisely by the help of the Holy Spirit, in Jesus' name.

3. I decree that every spirit of heaviness, torment, fear, or suicidal thought flees from my life by the authority in the name of Jesus, in Jesus' name.

4. I decree that I am not mentally unstable or

bound, I walk in divine sanity, clarity, and emotional strength, in Jesus' name.

5. I decree that every generational pattern of mental disorder is cancelled by the blood of Jesus, I belong to a new covenant, in Jesus' name.

6. I decree that my emotions are healed, my thoughts are renewed, and my heart is filled with the peace of God that surpasses understanding, in Jesus' name.

7. I decree that no label, diagnosis, or disorder has the final say over my life, Jehovah Rapha is my healer, in Jesus' name.

8. I decree that I am not a victim of confusion or torment, I am guarded by the peace of Christ and protected by divine wisdom, in Jesus' name.

9. I decree that any curse, word, or event that opened the door to mental affliction in my life is reversed and shut permanently, in Jesus' name.

10. I decree that I receive supernatural healing from every emotional wound, internal chaos, and mental anguish, in Jesus' name.

11. I decree that I break free from mental fog, panic attacks, and irrational fears, they shall not return again, in Jesus' name.

12. I decree that I am not insane, broken, or unstable, I am restored, renewed, and rooted in the truth of God's Word, in Jesus' name.

13. I decree that every medication and therapy I undergo is sanctified and used by God for my full recovery and restoration, in Jesus' name.

14. I decree that I no longer live under the weight

of mental exhaustion, nervous breakdowns, or identity crisis, I am whole, in Jesus' name.

15. I decree that God's divine light floods my mind, expelling all darkness, depression, and psychological bondage, in Jesus' name.

16. I decree that I have a calm, balanced, and healthy mind that produces good fruit, in Jesus' name.

17. I decree that the mental afflictions that affected others in my family line shall not affect me, I walk in divine exemption, in Jesus' name.

18. I decree that I am not ashamed of my journey, God is healing me and turning my scars into testimonies, in Jesus' name.

19. I decree that I will not lose my mind, identity, memory, or sense of purpose, God preserves me, in Jesus' name.

20. I decree that I shall live a joyful, productive, and mentally sound life, fully fulfilling destiny by the grace of God, in Jesus' name.

CHAPTER 47

Victory Over Shame and Disgrace

God is interested in the success of your business. He delights in the prosperity of His servants (Psalm 35:27), and He gives the power to get wealth (Deuteronomy 8:18). If your business has faced stagnation, losses, or consistent setbacks, it's time to rise in spiritual authority and decree and declare a divine turnaround. The marketplace is not just a financial arena; it is a platform for kingdom influence and expansion.

Your business is more than just a source of income; it is a divine assignment. God desires to bless the work of your hands, give you divine ideas, connect you to Favor, and make you a channel of His provision. Every curse of failure, limitation, or delay working against your business must be broken. Every closed door must open, and every dry season must give way to abundance.

Declare the Favor of God over your business, staff, customers, and operations. Speak life into your finances. Ask the Lord for divine strategies, marketing wisdom, and new opportunities. As you decree breakthrough, expect angelic assistance and supernatural interventions that no human effort can produce.

This is your season for contracts, expansions, new clients, visibility, and wealth transfer. Do not let fear or past losses hinder your faith. You are partnering with Jehovah Jireh, the God who provides and multiplies.

Speak boldly. Believe fully. Watch God do the impossible.

Key Scriptures:

- Deuteronomy 8:18 "But you shall remember the Lord your God, for it is He who gives you power to get wealth..."
- Psalm 90:17 "Let the beauty of the Lord our God be upon us, and establish the work of our hands for us..."
- Job 22:28 "You shall also decree a thing, and it shall be established for you..."

Prophetic Declarations

1. I decree that every garment of shame placed upon my life is consumed by the fire of God and replaced with a robe of honour, in Jesus' name.

2. I decree that public humiliation and secret reproach shall no longer be my portion, for the Lord has crowned me with glory, in Jesus' name.

3. I decree that those who mocked me will witness my divine elevation, and the name of the Lord shall be glorified in my life, in Jesus' name.

4. I decree that every disgrace assigned to destroy my reputation is reversed and turned into a testimony of honour and Favor, in Jesus' name.

5. I decree that I walk in boldness and not in

shame, for the Lord has taken away my reproach and restored my dignity, in Jesus' name.

6. I decree that every insult and accusation meant to break me is turning around to promote me by the power of God, in Jesus' name.

7. I decree that I am honoured where I was once rejected, celebrated where I was once ignored, and lifted where I was once cast down, in Jesus' name.

8. I decree that every satanic plan to disgrace me publicly is exposed and nullified by the blood of Jesus, in Jesus' name.

9. I decree that shame will never be the end of my store, my end shall be glorious, beautiful, and full of praise, in Jesus' name.

10. I decree that every foundational reproach speaking against my name and destiny is silenced forever, in Jesus' name.

11. I decree that I am not forgotten or forsakes, I am divinely remembered for good and positioned for royal honour, in Jesus' name.

12. I decree that I arise from the ashes of disgrace into the palace of honour, for the Lord delights in my restoration, in Jesus' name.

13. I decree that divine beauty replaces every area of shame in my lift, my life shall radiate joy, grace, and victory, in Jesus' name.

14. I decree that every tongue that has risen to accuse, defame, or destroy me is condemned and silenced, in Jesus' name.

15. I decree that the mercy of God speaks louder

than the mistakes of my pass, my story is being rewritten in grace, in Jesus' name.

16. I decree that the years of disgrace are over; a new season of recognition, elevation, and celebration begins for me, in Jesus' name.

17. I decree that God lifts my head above every circumstance that once caused me to hang it in shame, in Jesus' name.

18. I decree that the presence of God shields me from public shame and covers me with divine Favor, in Jesus' name.

19. I decree that every mockery against my life turns into a miracle that announces the faithfulness of God, in Jesus' name.

20. I decree that I walk in perpetual honour, clothed with divine confidence and radiant with the glory of God, in Jesus' name.

CHAPTER 48

Freedom from Occult Attacks

Many battles in life have spiritual roots. Occult powers, whether engaged knowingly or unknowingly, open doors to dark spiritual influences that can bring fear, bondage, affliction, confusion, and delay. But as a child of God, you have been delivered from the power of darkness and translated into the kingdom of His dear Son (Colossians 1:13). It is your right to walk in total freedom.

Occult attacks can manifest through nightmares, sudden misfortunes, mental torment, unexplainable illnesses, or demonic oppression. These attacks often originate from ancestral altars, secret initiations, rituals, or ungodly covenants, sometimes even from previous generations. But the power of the cross is greater than any curse or ritual. You must rise to decree and declare your total deliverance from all occultic oppression in Jesus' name.

Through the name of Jesus, the blood of Jesus, and the Word of God, you can break free from every yoke of darkness. As you begin to declare freedom, you are invoking divine authority that scatters every evil gathering and silences every enchantment.

Every spell, charm, and incantation are rendered powerless under the fire of God. God's Word is your sword. Speak it. Believe it. And walk in your liberty. This is your season to break every ungodly tie, cancel every evil ordinance, and reclaim your life and destiny.

Decree and declare boldly. You are not a victim, you are victorious!

Key Scriptures:

- Colossians 1:13 "He has delivered us from the power of darkness and conveyed us into the kingdom of the Son of His love."
- Isaiah 54:17 "No weapon formed against you shall prosper..."
- Job 22:28 "You shall also decree a thing, and it shall be established for you..."

Prophetic Declarations

1. I decree that every occult assignment, ritual, and incantation targeting my life is destroyed by the power in the name of Jesus, in Jesus' name.

2. I decree that no weapon formed through witchcraft, sorcery, divination, or enchantment shall prosper against me or my household, in Jesus' name.

3. I decree that I am covered by the fire of the Holy Ghost, and every occult surveillance or spiritual monitoring is consumed by that fire, in Jesus' name.

4. I decree that my name, photo, voice, or possessions cannot be used for evil manipulation or spiritual control, in Jesus' name.

5. I decree that every demonic sacrifice or blood ritual carried out against my destiny is rendered null and void by the blood of Jesus, in Jesus' name.

6. I decree that I am disconnected from every spiritual altar of darkness where my name, future, or family has been invoked, in Jesus' name.

7. I decree that every evil hand stretched toward me from the camp of darkness withers now and loses its hold, in Jesus' name.

8. I decree that every form of astral projection, soul tie, or evil visitation through dreams or trances is permanently cut off from my life, in Jesus' name.

9. I decree that I walk in the light of Christ and no shadow of darkness or occultic initiation can cover or influence me, in Jesus' name.

10. I decree that the power of the Most High overthrows every occult covenant, secret pact, or spiritual initiation done knowingly or unknowingly on my behalf, in Jesus' name.

11. I decree that every voice of enchantment, spell, or charm speaking against my mind, peace, or health is silenced now, in Jesus' name.

12. I decree that I am hidden in Christ, far above principalities and powers, no evil force from the underworld can reach me, in Jesus' name.

13. I decree that my spirit, soul, and body are saturated with divine immunity against any spiritual poison, occult oppression, or demonic

influence, in Jesus' name.

14. I decree that I am surrounded by the fire of God day and night; no occultic power can penetrate the hedge of divine protection, in Jesus' name.

15. I decree that every strange sickness, confusion, or affliction released through occult arrows is reversed back to the sender, in Jesus' name.

16. I decree that the Lord arises and scatters every coven, gathering, or conclave where my destiny is being discussed or tampered with, in Jesus' name.

17. I decree that every demonic chain used to bind my destiny, joy, or progress is broken by the anointing, in Jesus' name.

18. I decree that I belong to Jesus, spirit, soul, and body, and no other power has a legal right over my life, in Jesus' name.

19. I decree that I am surrounded by warring angels and the blood of Jesus; no occultic power can cross the boundary of my life, in Jesus' name.

20. I decree that the victory of the cross is final and total over my life, and I walk daily in freedom from all occult powers, in Jesus' name.

CHAPTER 49

Divine Helpers

In the journey of destiny, no one succeeds alone. Even Jesus had help in fulfilling His earthly assignment, Simon of Cyrene carried His cross (Mark 15:21). Divine helpers are God-ordained individuals strategically positioned to assist, support, speak on your behalf, and connect you to the next phase of your destiny. Without them, delay, frustration, and stagnation can set in.

Many breakthroughs require a "man sent from God." Your divine helper could be a mentor, an intercessor, a sponsor, a gatekeeper, or even a stranger. These are people who obey God's prompting to open doors, give counsel, offer resources, or fight battles on your behalf. When divine helpers arise, obstacles crumble and miracles happen.

But sometimes, demonic interference blocks your helpers. Wicked spirits release confusion, suspicion, or distance between you and those sent to lift you. That is why it's not enough to wait passively, you must decree and declare the release and alignment of your divine helpers by the authority of the name of Jesus.

This chapter equips you to call forth the right people and reject the wrong ones. You will declare open heavens over your connections and pray for discernment to recognize those assigned to your life.

Declare boldly: My helpers will locate me. My destiny shall not suffer delay. I receive divine assistance without sorrow or manipulation, in Jesus' name.

Key Scriptures:

- Isaiah 46:11 "Indeed I have spoken it; I will also bring it to pass. I have purposed it; I will also do it."
- Psalm 121:2 "My help comes from the Lord, who made heaven and earth."
- Job 22:28 "You shall also decree a thing, and it shall be established for you…"

Prophetic Declarations

1. I decree that divine helpers arise for me in every season and location to assist me in fulfilling God's purpose for my life, in Jesus' name.
2. I decree that I will not be stranded or helpless, God has assigned men and women to lift, support, and Favor me, in Jesus' name.
3. I decree that every helper of my destiny, whether spiritual, financial, or governmental, locates me speedily and without delay, in Jesus' name.
4. I decree that I will not miss my divine connections, God orders my steps into places of Favor, support, and strategic relationships, in Jesus' name.
5. I decree that I am not invisible or ignored, my name, face, and work are brought to the remembrance of those sent to help me, in Jesus' name.
6. I decree that every demonic veil covering me from my divine helpers is torn apart by the fire

of the Holy Ghost, in Jesus' name.

7. I decree that my destiny helpers are released from every spiritual cage, delay, or distraction, and they locate me now, in Jesus' name.

8. I decree that I am not rejected, forgotten, or disqualified, God uses even unlikely people to be a blessing to me, in Jesus' name.

9. I decree that I am surrounded by people who love righteousness, walk in truth, and are assigned to help carry out God's plan for my life, in Jesus' name.

10. I decree that I receive Favor in high places, open doors through the hands of divine helpers, and mercy from unexpected sources, in Jesus' name.

11. I decree that divine helpers are positioned in every season of my lift, no matter where I go, help follows me, in Jesus' name.

12. I decree that I do not suffer in silence or struggle in the dark, God sends destiny angels in human form to lift me up, in Jesus' name.

13. I decree that my helpers will not be manipulated, delayed, or diverted, they are drawn to me by the hand of God, in Jesus' name.

14. I decree that I walk in divine alignment with those who are assigned to teach, mentor, finance, elevate, and announce me, in Jesus' name.

15. I decree that I will not labour in vain or build alone, God surrounds me with skilful, faithful, and helpful hands, in Jesus' name.

16. I decree that even strangers rise up to help me,

and kings respond to the call of my destiny, in Jesus' name.

17. I decree that every helper assigned to my calling, business, ministry, or family comes forth without delay, in Jesus' name.

18. I decree that the hearts of my helpers are stirred by the Holy Spirit, they will not rest until they fulfil their assignment concerning me, in Jesus' name.

19. I decree that I am a magnet of divine help, where others are refused, I am remembered, recommended, and rewarded, in Jesus' name.

20. I decree that divine help is my covenant portion, I will never walk alone or fall unnoticed, for God has appointed helpers for my journey, in Jesus' name.

CHAPTER 50

Sealing and Covering with the Blood of Jesus

There is no greater protection, covering, or seal than the Blood of Jesus Christ. It is not merely symbolic; it is a spiritual weapon that speaks, covers, defends, and delivers. In the face of danger, demonic attack, accusation, and judgment, the Blood stands as your divine shield. It marks you as untouchable to the forces of darkness.

When the Israelites were instructed to apply the blood of the lamb on their doorposts, it wasn't a religious ritual, it was a life-saving instruction. "When I see the blood, I will pass over you..." (Exodus 12:13). That blood was a shadow; today, we have the real thing, the Blood of the eternal Lamb, Jesus Christ.

You must learn to decree and declare the covering of the Blood over your life, family, property, purpose, and everything connected to you. When you apply the Blood in faith, you neutralize curses, silence accusations, frustrate evil agendas, and establish divine security.

This final chapter empowers you to close every open door, seal every breakthrough, and frustrate every monitoring spirit. You will invoke the Blood to create a barrier against affliction, misfortune, and retaliation from the enemy.

Your victories must be sealed. Your testimony must be preserved. Your tomorrow must be covered.

Declare with authority: I decree the Blood of Jesus seals my life, my destiny, and all that concerns me. No power of hell can overturn what God has done in me, in Jesus' name.

Key Scriptures:

- Revelation 12:11 "And they overcame him by the blood of the Lamb and by the word of their testimony..."
- Exodus 12:13 "When I see the blood, I will pass over you..."
- Job 22:28 "You shall also decree a thing, and it shall be established for you..."
-

Prophetic Declarations

1. I decree that I am sealed by the blood of Jesus, and no evil force, curse, or attack can penetrate the divine hedge around my life, in Jesus' name.

2. I decree that the blood of Jesus marks my home, my family, and my possessions, no plague or disaster shall come near me, in Jesus' name.

3. I decree that every evil monitoring spirit, demonic assignment, or spiritual arrow is rendered powerless by the blood of Jesus, in Jesus' name.

4. I decree that every door of access to the enemy is closed by the power of the blood, I am covered,

protected, and shielded, in Jesus' name.

5. I decree that the blood of Jesus speaks better things over my life, mercy, healing, breakthrough, and deliverance, in Jesus' name.

6. I decree that my mind, body, and spirit are purified, renewed, and preserved by the cleansing power of the blood of Jesus, in Jesus' name.

7. I decree that every covenant contrary to God's will is nullified by the eternal covenant of the blood of Jesus, in Jesus' name.

8. I decree that the blood of Jesus silences every voice of accusation and condemnation speaking against me in the spirit realm, in Jesus' name.

9. I decree that I overcome every demonic battle, temptation, and affliction through the blood of the Lamb and the word of my testimony, in Jesus' name.

10. I decree that the blood of Jesus cancels every death sentence, sickness, delay, and generational curse in my life, in Jesus' name.

11. I decree that the blood of Jesus shields me in the day and covers me in the night, no evil shall befall me, in Jesus' name.

12. I decree that my journey, my rising, my ministry, and my destiny are preserved and empowered by the blood of Jesus, in Jesus' name.

13. I decree that the blood of Jesus stands as a divine barrier between me and any form of spiritual manipulation or witchcraft, in Jesus' name.

14. I decree that my finances, my marriage, my

children, and my health are sealed from satanic interference by the blood of Jesus, in Jesus' name.

15. I decree that I walk daily under the covering of the blood, safeguarded from accidents, evil decisions, and untimely death, in Jesus' name.

16. I decree that every legal right the enemy claim over my life is revoked and overturned by the blood of Jesus, in Jesus' name.

17. I decree that I am untouchable, unmovable, and undefeatable because I dwell under the covering of the blood of Jesus, in Jesus' name.

18. I decree that as I go out and come in, the blood of Jesus goes before me, surrounds me, and fights for me, in Jesus' name.

19. I decree that I am eternally secured, spiritually hidden, and divinely favoured under the blood covenant of Jesus Christ, in Jesus' name.

20. I decree that the blood of Jesus will continue to speak for me, cover me, and guarantee my total victory in every battle, in Jesus' name.

Closing Word

As you've journeyed through these prophetic declarations, know this: your voice carries authority, your words have weight, and your faith is a force that heaven responds to. You are no longer a silent spectator of life; you are a bold degree of divine destiny.

The Word of God in your mouth is not empty. It is living, active, and sharper than any two-edged sword (Hebrews 4:12). Each time you opened your mouth and declared these prophetic truths, something shifted in the spirit realm, even if you haven't seen it yet. Heaven is moving, angels are working, and the power of the Holy Spirit is backing every declaration with signs and wonders.

Remember: persistence is key. Keep declaring until your reality aligns with God's Word. Speak life until dead things resurrect. Decree breakthrough until the walls fall. Proclaim freedom until every chain is broken. There is power in repetition, power in consistency, and power in unwavering faith.

Let this book be a lifelong companion, a manual for victory, a guide for intercession, and a springboard for transformation. Revisit each chapter when you feel weak, under attack, uncertain, or when you simply want to reinforce your position in Christ. You are seated in heavenly places, and your declarations should reflect that authority.

Do not stop declaring. Do not stop believing. And never underestimate what happens when a child of God opens their mouth in faith.

Continue to decree and watch what God will establish.

May every word you've spoken manifest swiftly, powerfully, and gloriously, in Jesus' name. Amen.

Final Prayer of Activation

Heavenly Father,

Thank You for the grace and revelation released through this journey of prophetic declarations. I stand today not just as a reader, but as a royal priest and a prophetic voice, ready to speak forth Your will on the earth.

Lord, I activate every word I have declared in faith. Let

these declarations rise before You as incense and let answers break forth speedily. I align my life with Your promises, and I silence every contrary voice of doubt, fear, delay, and defeat.

I decree that my tongue is anointed to speak life, shift atmospheres, and command divine results. I receive divine boldness to continue decreeing until manifestation comes. Let every dry bone live, every closed door open, every barrier break, and every chain be shattered.

Father, I step into my inheritance. I declare that every area of my life is now under the government of the Holy Spirit. I am no longer a victim of circumstances, but a vessel of power and glory. My home, my health, my purpose, my destiny, my ministry, and my generations are all sealed with the blood of Jesus and aligned with divine purpose.

I receive fresh fire, renewed faith, and unstoppable momentum to keep declaring what You have spoken. I decree that I shall testify, and others shall see the results of prophetic utterances and give glory to You.

Thank You, Father, for Your Word that never returns void. Let it be done according to my declarations, in Jesus' mighty name. Amen.

ABOUT THE AUTHOR

Francisca Okeya is a prophetic intercessor, author, and passionate teacher of God's Word, divinely called to equip and empower believers through bold prayers, prophetic declarations, and uncompromising biblical truth. She carries a unique grace to awaken spiritual authority in the lives of others and guide them into the fullness of their God-ordained purpose.

With a deep burden for deliverance, healing, and restoration, Francisca has written extensively on spiritual growth, breakthrough, and prayer. Her Spirit-led teachings and prophetic writings have touched lives, breaking strongholds, igniting faith, restoring hope, and drawing hearts into deeper intimacy with the Holy Spirit.

She serves faithfully at The Redeemed Assemblies (The Blessed Church) as a servant-leader in both pulpit ministry and intercession. Through various platforms, she continues to equip the body of Christ to speak life, shift atmospheres, and establish heaven's will on earth through the power of the spoken word.

Francisca is also a prolific author, known for producing spiritually empowering books designed to transform lives, renew minds, and strengthen faith. Her titles include:

- Prayer Rainfall: Prayers That Touch Heaven and Shake the Earth

A powerful collection of Spirit-inspired, targeted

prayers for intercessors, warriors, and those contending for breakthrough.

- Healing Belongs to You: Receiving What Christ Paid for at the Cross

An in-depth revelation on how to receive, walk in, and maintain divine healing through the finished work of Jesus.

- The Ministry of the Holy Spirit: God in Us Understanding the Ministry of the Holy Spirit

A 31-chapter teaching guide that unveils the person, presence, and purpose of the Holy Spirit in every believer's life.

- Decree and Be Established: Prophetic Declarations for Every Area of Life

A treasury of prophetic declarations to speak over your life, family, purpose, and future, unlocking the creative power of words.

- Peace for the Troubled Mind: A Journey of Emotional and Mental Healing

A practical and biblical roadmap to emotional wholeness, helping readers overcome anxiety, depression, and fear through God's Word.

- Holy Spirit Academy: Embracing Divine Training for Spiritual Growth

A discipleship manual for those desiring to be mentored by the Holy Spirit and grow into spiritual maturity and many more.

To learn more or get in touch, contact: info@cyska.com

Printed in Dunstable, United Kingdom

67269306R00127